Lilian Bell

A little Sister to the Wilderness

Lilian Bell

A little Sister to the Wilderness

ISBN/EAN: 9783337139070

Printed in Europe, USA, Canada, Australia, Japan

Cover: Foto ©ninafisch / pixelio.de

More available books at **www.hansebooks.com**

A Little Sister to the Wilderness

BY

Lilian Bell

CHICAGO
STONE & KIMBALL
MDCCCXCV

TO
GEORGE C. LORIMER, D. D., LL. D.,

MY GENTLEST CRITIC AND MOST
INDULGENT FRIEND, THIS BOOK
IS AFFECTIONATELY DEDICATED.

Preface.

OUT of a personal regard for that most patient, long-suffering body of people in the world, the American public, I have been at some pains to remove all of the dialect from this simple tale that I could justify myself in doing. Everything difficult or obscure which naturally belongs to it, is safe in my waste-basket. And I have thus carefully prepared this expunged edition that the wayfaring man, though a fool, might not err therein.

Certain curious isolated cases of capacity amounting almost to genius, and of vice amounting almost to insanity, can only be explained by atavism. Aside from this, however, in attempting to portray the character of Mag, I have been led by the cry of the inarticulate, of that large, not-to-be-ignored portion of humanity, whose thoughts need an interpreter; who, with womanish, nice perceptions, need equally nice distinction in terms, to enable them to express the fine shades of meaning which it is their gift to feel. They belong to that vast majority of people who are only capable of lofty beginnings, who, when you have taken pity on their hesitation and finished their sentences for them, cry out to you in their gratitude that you have expressed with potent exactness, what they, in their impotence, could only feel.

To all such, be their yearning honest, can a proper vehicle be obtained by cultivation. Nor need this be feared as inducing garrulousness. Cultivation does not change traits; it only develops. The great soft gift of silence will always remain the precious possession of those who cherish it as they should. They shall still, as friend and mate, draw to themselves the articulate. And when, after many tossings to and fro, and much secret bitterness of spirit, they have at last found a form of expression for their lives, lo, in the perfect fulfilment of God's plan, shall they find their speech as unfettered as their spirit.

Chapter I.

IN THE WEST TENNESSEE BOTTOM-LAND.

MAG disliked to drive the mules, they were so vicious. She sat very straight, with her eyes upon their wicked ears. Her wagon had seen much hard usage, and she was respectful of its age and feebleness. The harness too did not hold out great promise of allegiance. Like some people's religion, it was not meant to stand a strain.

The road had deep gullies on each side, gullies which every rain made deeper, and whose worst places were filled with underbrush. It behooved Mag to drive carefully and let the mules set their own pace. Nevertheless there were urgent reasons why she ought to hurry. After going up to Henley's for her father and mother, there was the levee to be crossed. It was moonlight in the almanac or experienced Bottomites like the Manley family would never have risked crossing the levee after dark. But an ominous bank of clouds was creeping slowly out of the east, threatening to make the moonlight only one more of the almanac's broken promises.

In a foreboding of what lay before her, should she find that her father's convivial friends at "the store" had incapacitated him for driving, Mag could not resist flapping the reins a little, woman-fashion, and finding no effect followed such civility, she ventured to use the whip. To this, however, Old Nick promptly responded by a lively tattoo with his heels upon the tender singletree. While engaged in getting his mind off these unwelcome gymnastics, Mag saw, in the woods at her left,

Ralph Patterson, with a drove of hogs. Now if there was one thing that Old Nick especially detested, it was a hog. Mag, aware of this genteel prejudice, redoubled her efforts to induce him to press forward, but with a perversity almost human in its unreasonableness, Old Nick took this time to balk stubbornly.

Ralph espied Mag with a sudden dilating of his whole awkward being. He straightened himself, gave his hat a pull over his eyes, and with a dexterous movement, he swept the whole drove down into the gully just where it was deepest. There they would be safe for the time he meant to spend talking to Mag.

"Howdy, Mag!" he called out to her. But Mag was too anxiously watching Old Nick to answer him.

When the hogs, grunting in their most obnoxious fashion, pushed and crowded each other in the deep narrow gully, Old Nick pointed his ears forward suspiciously. Then he bunched his four feet together, and whirling swiftly on this improvised pivot, he bit the other mule on the back and kicked viciously. The cloud of dust covered Mag and the wagon and Ralph, but as it slowly settled white and hot, Old Nick could be seen, with his long ugly lips drawn back from his teeth, squealing with mulish insistence.

Mag wasted no time, but climbed down without speaking and fearlessly went to examine the harness.

"Keep away thom that air mule," cried Ralph, bounding up from the gully to where she stood. He seized Old Nick by the bit and most urgently jerked him around into place. Mag surveyed the ruin in silence, and Ralph stood watching with eyes full of dumb, helpless longing. Finally she looked at him.

"Why don't you help me splice this

rope?" she said. "You have belated me, so's we won't get home till midnight."

"*I* didn't do nothin'," he answered eagerly, trying to help her.

"You drove them hogs down into the gully when you know as well as I do that Old Nick won't stand hogs, no way you can fix 'em," she said, referring to this rooted prejudice of his as respectfully as if he had been a Jew.

"I forgot about him, I did for a fact. Don't feel bad about it, Mag, I'll fix it for you. I ain't talked to you for so long. You keep so fur away. 'Pears like you won't never let me get in spoke retch if you kin get out of it."

Mag made no answer.

Ralph suddenly dropped the rope he was splicing, and a dull fury flamed into his face.

"Who all air at Henley's that you air so powerful uneasy to get there?" he demanded jealously.

Mag knew that he was thinking of Ben Green, who generally was to be found at "the store." She resented the indelicacy on her part that his suspicion implied. In secret she held herself so proudly above being capable of such a thing that she would not even defend herself. Ralph mistook her silence.

"Mag Manley," he said, determined to speak, now that he had the opportunity, "Why air you so different from other girls? You ackchilly ack as if a boy was insultin' of you when he tries to court you. I thought girls liked to be courted. But you air that still, I don't understand you. You never give me a kine word or even a kine look. You make me feel like I was a yaller dawg meachin' along in your road. Ef it air Ben Green who is ahead of me, ef it air Ben Green—" He paused menacingly. Red lights came into his brown eyes.

Mag's surprised look disconcerted

him. He never had said so much before. Mag still worked over the harness. She said nothing.

Ralph stooped and took up the rope again, but he only held it idly. Mag finished hers, and walked around and drew his out of his nerveless hand.

"Won't you say something, Mag?"

"I can't think of anything to say to a boy who asks if Mag Manley is going to Henley's, because Ben Green might be there."

Ralph, like most men, overlooked the grave mistake that she was explicit enough to point out to him, in his delight to find his jealousy unfounded.

"You tell me for sollum shore it aint Ben?" he said eagerly.

Mag gave him the long, wondering, incredulous look, which a woman gives her lover, when she has tried to make him understand her for his own good, and he has obtusely ignored her generosity.

"For solemn sure," she answered so gravely that he ought to have known.

"Nor no other boy?" he persisted stupidly.

"Nor no other boy."

Even if his cause had not been hopeless before, Ralph had successfully extinguished it during this brief interview.

They worked in silence until the harness was mended. Ralph's plain, honest face was quivering and tremulous with hope. He looked at Mag's beauty in adoration. She was vainly seeking to convey to him that she was not thinking of him either, when they heard a wagon approaching.

"There's your Maw and Paw with the Johnsons," said Ralph.

"Yes. I was going after them. I reckon they got tired of waiting."

Mag thought he would regret his suspicions now surely, but instead he only answered:

"So it wasn't Ben, shore enough!"

"Mag," screamed her mother when they drew near enough to exchange into their own wagon.

"Yes'm."

"What on earth belated you so? Did them mules act up?"

"Yes'm."

"I'm glad it was only that. I was so bothered, I come along the road a piece to meet you. I couldn't help thinkin' of quicksands."

"Well, good-bye to y'all," said the Johnsons, "hope you'll get over the levee all right."

"Good-bye. We're 'bleeged to you fur bringin' us along."

The two wagons went on their way.

Ralph was left behind with the ungracious task of getting his hogs up out of the gully, but his simple soul was filled with the delight of having had such an interview with Mag. He looked anxiously at the cloudy sky as he thought of her long and dangerous journey.

Quicksands abound in West Tennessee, and it is best for a stranger to follow the road closely, even when it swings far to the left or right, and leaves an innocent bit of ground in the straight course, without a wheel track. The river-bottom is especially treacherous in summer, and often impassable in winter. So the levee, an elevated road built of logs, and partaking of the nature of a bridge, is the safest thoroughfare across the low grounds.

It has an insidious beginning of only a few logs laid together over a depression in the road. Then perhaps a small bridge spans an abrupt turn of the creek, and then a sudden drop in the river bed, where the country slopes downward from all the rest, makes of the levee a trestle, sometimes twenty feet above ground. Here it winds in and out through the trees, whose branches shade its sides, but whose roots are deep down by the edge of the creek, forming an airy drive on a level with the birds' nests.

It is without handrails and so narrow, however, that a wagon has only a terrifying margin on each side, and two could in no wise pass each other, save on the broad platforms, called bridges, placed for this purpose at certain distances apart. Here it is the custom for drivers to stop and listen for the sounds of any vehicle which may be approaching from an opposite direction. The predicament of their coming face to face does not occur as often as one might suppose, for the reason that horses' hoofs make no inconsiderable noise in the unbroken stillness of the bottomland, and it is only during the progress of a thunderstorm that this is likely to occur.

As this wagon reached the first bridge, darkness descended like a blanket, but the mules, accustomed to the etiquette of the levee, stopped of their own accord.

"Go awn, Mag," said the voice of old Tobe Manley, from the body of the wagon where he lay at ease. "No one aint out to-night."

His shriveled wife, yellow from chills and quinine, leaned forward on the front seat, with her elbows on her knees, smoking a cob-pipe. Mag sat beside her mother, gazing with growing uneasiness at the black clouds, a feeling in no wise shared by either of her parents, fatalists like many of their class.

In obedience to her father's lazy mandate, she flapped the patched reins up and down on the mules' backs. All entreaties and flappings, however, they ignored with the superb scorn of which only a mule is complete master.

"Go 'long!" shouted Mag, standing up.

Still they stood with down-hung heads and restless tails. Tobe lifted himself from his recumbent position and swore a most horrible string of oaths at them. They raised their ears expectantly, and then, as if having received what they were waiting for, they craned their necks forward and the wagon creaked on. Mag sat down. Tobe dropped back to his place. The excitement was over.

"It air goin' to rain afore we git home," remarked Mrs. Manley, removing her pipe from between her long, yellow teeth and expectorating with great precision of aim at the off mule.

"That aint thunder this time—it's a run-away," said Mag, leaning forward anxiously. They were not upon the highest part of the levee, but they were midway between two bridges and the intense darkness was only lifted by the lightning.

They all listened.

"Shore 'nuff," drawled Tobe, climbing down.

Mag sprang over the wheel and ran forward, not knowing what lay before her. She heard her mother following. The lightning played in broad clear flashes, and the thunder mingled itself with the rumble of the approaching vehicle. Mag stooped and listened. The hoof-beats were those of a horse, not a mule. There was scarcely any sound of wheels, therefore it was not a wagon, hardly a buggy.

"It must be that little yellow cart of the surveyor," said Mag. "His colt aint used to the levee. He's running anyhow."

She heard the furious squeal of a mule back of her.

"Laws-a-mercy!" cried Mrs. Manley in great excitement. "Listen at that! Ol' Nick's actin' up again and Paw aint got time to projeck with him and git him to listen to reason. If he balks and Paw has to leave him there, and this horse don't stop, there'll be a collision that'll knock everything into kingdom come! We'll all be killed, every last one of us! You wait an' see ef we aint!"

Mag fully realized her own danger. She heard the terrifying sounds of the runaway coming nearer and nearer, and the raised voice of her father arguing angrily with Old Nick. Mag's heart pounded heavily against her side, and something was choking her.

The runaway was almost upon them, but she never thought of saving herself. Her mother was scuttling back and forth in a frenzy of fear. Mag stood as near to the edge of the levee as she dared, and shouted at the top of her strong young voice. Mrs. Manley shrieked and fled. The horse reared at the sounds, plunged forward and stumbled. Mag heard him fall upon his knees. Then as the lightning sent a strong glare, she sprang for him and seized his bit, not one minute too soon, for as he recovered himself, he swung her completely off her feet, just as his driver came to her rescue.

"How brave of you!" he said, speaking in a deep powerful voice whose like Mag never had heard before.

"Oh no," she said deprecatingly.

"I never saw a braver act," he reiterated.

"It was nothing," returned Mag, in some confusion.

"Mag!" screamed her mother, "did you cotch him?"

"Yes'm."

Mrs. Manley fluttered near.

"And you aint killed?"

"No'm."

"Aint nobody hurt?"

"No'm."

The horse was still stamping and snorting with terror, but Mag seemed to have no intention of loosing her valiant hold. Mrs. Manley kept well out of the way, but her voice cut the darkness like a saw.

Mag, with her keen forester training, had been right in her shrewd surmise that it was the surveyor's little thoroughbred, but the tall stranger standing opposite to her was not young Mr. Addison.

"Do let me hold him alone, and you stand further away," he urged.

"Oh, Mag can hold him," cried her mother, "but this aint no kind of a place for two teams to meet and a storm comin' awn."

Camden in the flickering light could see the thin silhouette of Mrs. Manley and the regally tall figure of the younger woman.

"How come you to be drivin' Mr. Addison's horse?" demanded Mrs. Manley with a shrill note of suspicion in her voice.

"My own went lame, and I felt that I must get to 'the store' to-night. My name is Camden. Addison begged me to stay over night with him, but I felt a call to go forward that very hour and I came."

The deep seriousness of his last words thrilled Mag, for she too, was used to listen to inward voices, and to follow the beckoning of invisible hands. His name brought no significance to either of them, but if he had said he was the preacher whom they were expecting to lead their protracted meeting, they would have known instantly.

The sound of dragging chains and frightful oaths startled him.

"What is that?" he asked, half indignantly.

"It's only Paw," volunteered Mrs. Manley glibly. "I reckon he's hitchin' Gineral Grant to the tail-eend of the wagon and haulin' it back to the bridge, so's y' all can git by."

The gaunt shape of the other mule standing near, moved restlessly and Camden stepped towards him, but Mrs.

Manley laid a bony, detaining hand on his arm.

"You want to git killed?" she asked, "Nary mules in West Tennessee kicks like Ol' Nick an' Gineral Grant. They air ugly as sin an' mean as dirt. Paw, he named 'em that-a-way 'case he says all the trouble the South ever had come from one or t'other of them two. He gits a power o' comfort out of swearin' at 'em as he is 'bleeged to do constant."

"He wouldn't have kicked me from that side," said Camden.

"That air mule don't kick 'cordin' to no rule," observed Mrs. Manley, grimly.

Camden desisted and turned back to his own horse, which was becoming unmanageable again. Suddenly the thunder concentrated all its fury and rent the heavens in one ear-splitting crash. The terrified horse sprang to one side and disappeared off the levee. The shock as he jerked his bit from Mag's hand sent her reeling against Camden, who steadied them both.

"Are you hurt?" he cried anxiously, realizing more and more how Mag had imperiled herself.

"No," she said hurriedly. "Listen."

They heard the horse struggle and the snapping of broken shafts and harness. Mrs. Manley who had again made for the safety of her husband, was crying frantically for protection from the thunder.

"He isn't killed," said Mag. "Listen. He's walking off. Maybe he isn't hurt. But the cart is plumb ruined. It sounded like kindlin' wood."

"I don't care about the cart, but are you sure about the horse?"

"Why, yes; can't you hear him?"

"I can hear nothing, but I trust you. Now tell me how I can get to him."

"Are you studyin' about goin' tonight?"

"Indeed I am. I must give up trying to reach Henley's. I shall go after the horse and then go back to Addison's. He wanted me to stay with him but I was led here."

Mag understood him far better than he knew, but she only said,

"I'll call Paw. He can tell you what to do. Don't try to pass Old Nick. He don't mind me."

Mag left Camden standing there and slipped past the mule without difficulty. She sent Tobe to confer with Camden and climbed to her place in the wagon beside her mother. Presently Tobe came back leading Old Nick, and proceeded to harness him again in the safety of the bridge.

"That air city fellow is a plumb fool," he remarked under his breath. "Mag, you air more of a man than him, —slim little saplin'—could n't you have cotched that hoss 'fore he went over?"

"That wasn't Mr. Addison," she

answered. "He gave out his name to be Camden, but it was the surveyor's horse. Mr. Camden is twice as big as Mr. Addison."

"He give me five dollars to go after the hoss and made it ten if I would go to-night. I did n't recollect to tell him I 'd a-gone as quick fur seventy-five cents. I told him it was too durn fur, but he said the hoss might be hurt and I must go. He do n't know the way. I tole him I reckoned the hoss was killed."

"Well, I know he aint killed," said Mag, "nor hurt bad 'cause I made out to hear him walking off."

"Then you 've spoilt my game," said Tobe angrily. "I knowed the hoss was n't hurt, too, but I was n't fool enough to tell him when he said he was comin' to pay me the other five to-morrah. I could a-doctored him for a month and made that fellow pay me for it. Now you 've ruined it all. Nor it aint like you to talk too much. You aint like yore Maw."

Mrs. Manley did not resent the insinuation. She chuckled at her old man's shrewd plans.

"Is he comin' to our house?" asked Mag timidly.

"Yes; but first, we air goin' to pick him up and tote him as fur as the levee eend."

His satisfied grin showed his thin blue lips and yellow teeth as he softly repeated,

"I'm thes shore he is a plumb fool."

Chapter II.

ON THE LEVEE.

DROPPING from the level rim of the country round about, to where through its lowliest center winds a thin silver stream, lie the low grounds of West Tennessee. Their sloping sides are hidden in a mass of jessamine and wild honeysuckle and columbine, until viewed from the levee which spans its treacherous bogs, it looks like a great bowl filled with a rainbow tangle of Southern bloom.

This view of summer beauty gives no hint of the devastating winter flood, when the sinuous windings of "The Creek" creep over its shifting banks and swollen with a slow, sullen rage crawl over reed and bush and tree until a yellow, sluggish sea has overcome the wilderness.

The shabby little farms of the poor whites, who live in these bottom-lands, are inundated partially if not wholly every year. Every year while the eager spring sun is drying out the land, the inhabitants are shaking in the mighty grasp of a malaria which, like their sloth, is an inheritance. The steam from the wet earth is like one tremendous washing-day and looks as though all creation had hung itself out to dry. Yet these people do not regard "The Creek" as their enemy. Their philosophy of life is simple. They accept the inevitable, whether of good or ill, with what in Attica might have been termed stoicism. In West Tennessee however, such an energetic term does not apply. Their sublime heights of indifference have been attained, have been foisted upon them rather, by generations of ancestral shiftlessness. Never, if they waded waist-deep in water, would they think of moving and bettering their condition. Malaria only lasts through the summer and the flood only lasts through the winter. They are always patiently waiting for a change of evils. They believe that nature will adjust herself if they but let her alone, and this is the one thing that they do with any degree of energy. Quinine is the sole assistance which they offer that nature which rules alike their crops and their aimless lives. Aside from this they leave her to work out her own salvation. Their one luxury, tobacco. Their one excitement, protracted meeting. Their one ailment, chills. Their motto, "Wait." Their creed, "I believe in Eternal Rest."

The Manley wagon overtook Camden on the levee, just as the first rain was beginning to fall. He was not at all surprised to see that Tobe intended to have him ride under shelter with himself and leave the women to drive and take full benefit of the rain.

He frustrated this unconscious selfishness with the tact which made Tobe flatter himself that he had intended the transformation all along.

"Come," Camden said to Mag, taking off his coat as he spoke, "you and your mother get back in there. Tobe and I are going to drive. Put your coat over your wife, and then cover them with this sacking. Such a rain will soon soak through everything."

The two women, accustomed to implicit obedience, obeyed the authority in Camden's voice, silently wondering how Tobe would like it. But Tobe felt the influence of a commanding presence as well as they, and hastened to follow Camden's example with a secret pleasure in a chivalry he had not intended, but which tingled in him like a thrill from his long forgotten past. He remembered with pride, how, when he was courting he used to do such things.

The rain came down in torrents and the darkness was so intense that all they could do was to let the mules pick their slow way and trust to their sagacity for safety.

Mrs. Manley stood the heat of her manifold coverings as long as she could. She put her head out cautiously.

"Whoo!" she said, "I kaint breathe under all this kiver. I'd ruther git soppin' wet than sweat to death without no reason and no sense in it, when air a-plenty is to be had, not even for the askin', but just for the sniffin'. I had to take this tender keer from your Paw when he was courtin' me, but I've done without it so long, I don't seem to take kindly to it. I feel 'sif I had a couple of feather beds awn me." She glanced up to where they could see the two figures of the men sitting bolt upright, getting full force of the driving rain.

"I don't believe they can see us," proceeded Mrs. Manley, cautiously putting out first one foot and then the other. "I would n't hurt your Paw's feelin's fur the world, but I got to breathe. Just put your hand out keerful and pull this sackin' away. I'm steamed like dumplin' and greens. Do n't you darst take yours off. That air fellow is made to be minded. He kivered you up and my advice is—stay kivered. Law-zee! If he 'd a-said in them thar thunder tones 'Mis. Manley, may I have the pleasure of seein' you ride Ol' Nick?' I'd a clumb awn that mewel if he'd a stood me awn my head for my impidence. His words air as easy as smilin', but his voice behind 'em says 'Git up an' dust.' So, Mag Manley, you stay kivered."

Mag, with her eyes luminous with an unknown feeling, had no intention of disobeying Camden. In him she had met, for the first time, one of the gentle folk whom she worshipped from afar. She watched them whenever she had the opportunity, admiring their quiet manners, their cultivated speech, the dainty clothes of the women, and trying to mould herself accordingly. Their courtesies to each other filled Mag's heart with an anguished yearning to be like them. Her quick ear, accustomed to listen for each separate bird note in the vast forest which was her school; her trained eye knowing the haunt of each tender green thing as it pushed its timid way into view in its appointed season, stood her in good stead when she studied men and women. And as it was native refinement struggling to express itself fittingly, it came to pass that her language was the last thing to adjust itself. So while compassing original thoughts evolved from her silent communion with the depths of the still forest, she was obliged to speak as others of her class spoke, who, as they watched her come and go among them, never dreamed that she differed in any way from themselves.

For the first time she had received one of these courtesies. It did not occur to her that she never had seen just this particular attention offered. To her mind there was nothing grotesque in the situation. In her simplicity she accepted the spirit of kindliness as the complete fulfilment of the highest courtesy, and never dreamed of the existence of that pitiful portion of humanity who demand only the outward form of politeness, and are ready with their cruel ridicule if this same form be not of the most finished outside, leaving the prompting spirit grieved and forgotten.

The rain ceased as suddenly as it had begun, and the clear, silver light from the repentant moon flooded the levee and the fragrant valley beneath it. Mrs. Manley slily drew the sacking up over her again, then sat up and threw it off with a great show of relief. Camden turned around and smiled down at them. His powerful figure stood out against the driven rainclouds, and beside it Tobe's bent form looked shrunken.

As they drew up before the house, Camden sprang down and held out his hands to Mrs. Manley. She hesitated a moment, then presented her elbows to him. He betrayed no surprise even beneath Mag's searching glance, but placed her in safety on the ground. As he reached up for Mag, there was one long moment as she leaned towards him in which their eyes met. For the first time Mag's inarticulate soul felt the personal nearness of a human being, one who thought and felt like herself, and one who spoke as she would speak if she could.

The only drawback to her pleasure was the fact that now their poverty would rise before him like a nightmare. Now he must see how pitiful their home was. He would see everything. But counteracting this was the incident of another courtesy at his hands. She had been handed down like a lady. Her mother served her father after the manner of an aboriginal squaw. If Mrs. Manley, in descending from their wagon, did not clamber over the wheel unassisted, Tobe reached for her and hauled her down with about the attention to detail that he would bestow upon a bale of cotton. At protracted meeting, Mag had watched with almost tearful eyes, the feathery way in which Miss Bettie Chisholm fluttered to the ground with the support of her cavalier's hand. She knew that among those people such things were an every-day occurrence. She did not dream that she would be one of that number, and never to the day of her death, did she forget the breathless thrill that shook her when Camden first offered them to her. They filled her with a new and strange exultation. She felt that they made a lady of her.

To Mag and her class the word lady meant everything. It symbolized every longing of her nature, for caste is nowhere more strongly defined than among these people. Her eager mind grew in spite of all restrictions, but grew wrongly of course, having no master. Words had a distorted significance to her from their constant misuse. She felt this, without being able to express it. Her knowledge was speech-locked, and he must possess a keen eye and a feminine intuition who could read her secret in her face. Beauty such as hers successfully masks unusual intelligence, for who looks for philosophy in Venus?

She possessed an innate refinement which shamed civilization. As she stood beside Camden for a moment in the white moonlight and saw him glance searchingly at the meager bare house, lifted high above ground to be out of the reach of the flood; then from her father and mother, limp and rainsoaked back to her, so straight and handsome with her brown bloom and shifting color, she felt his surprised thoughts. Mag was a human sensitive plant — an inarticulate soul-endogen. Perhaps from some remote ancestor she inherited a strain of blood which made a lady of her. Keen, fine intuitions, having no part in the make-up of her people, were hers from birth. She never had met anyone who dreamed that beneath that almost immutable silence of hers, lay a nature, rich, full, complete, waiting the approach of one whose sympathetic comprehension should be the key to unlock her lips and give them speech. Uncultured, untaught, she yet possessed the grander harmony of soul and poetry of heart which many masters and many tongues cannot teach to aught save the elect.

Mag never had been understood. She had looked upward into the bending sky with a glad sense of personal nearness that no human being ever had inspired. She had bestowed her passionate tenderness upon the pleading beauty of each slender tree and clinging vine. But as Camden brought his eyes from that comprehensive sweep of her surroundings, there flashed into Mag's the first look of sympathy which had ever stirred their luminous depths. And as he looked, he felt that those deep-seeing eyes, as yet only capable of making the dumb woodlands articulate, were destined to see into human souls.

Mag no longer dreaded to have him see their poverty. She no longer felt her mother's loquacity and her father's awkwardness. Even her own shortcomings melted into the background under the mantle of charity which Camden's glance flung over everything. She need not hide or pretend. He had arrayed himself on her side with a silent sympathy which trembled along her tense nerves to her finger-tips.

Tobe's voice interrupted her thoughts.

"I kin drive you awn just as well as not, and then go after yore hoss. It will be as light as day to-night."

"No, no indeed," returned Camden. "that light is the one you tell me is Addison's. I can find it alone. I can't begin to tell you how sorry I am for the trouble I've caused you, but I am very glad to have met you."

"Don't mention it," said Mrs. Manley, stepping up to him. "I do hate to have you go awn to-night. We'd be proper glad to have you stay with us till morning."

Once Mag would have shivered from this invitation as from a blow. Now she stood simply looking at him. When he turned to her, she smiled at him like a child. Camden did not see Tobe pluck at his wife's dress in vexed remonstrance. She twitched it from his grasp and moved her hand behind her back to signify that she understood.

"Oh no, Mrs. Manley. You are very kind, but I must get back to Addison. I hope you will be none the worse for getting wet."

"We air used to it," she responded. "It's been rainin' constant all summer. Crops is fine, almost too fine. So much rain makes 'em rot. I aint never seen such flowers in the Bottom since I lived here. My advice to you, bein' a stranger in these parts is — take quinine. 'T wont hurt you a mite. We air all goin' to take it."

"Thank you very much, Mrs. Manley. Good night."

"Good night," answered the Manleys.

Camden walked away towards the red light in Addison's window.

Chapter III.

THE MANLEY FAMILY AT HOME.

TO Camden's relief Addison took the bad news about the horse with calmness.

"You couldn't help it, old man," he said kindly. "He might have broken away from me, in just that way. You ought to be thankful that the whole thing wasn't spoiled by having the lovely girl lacking, or don't preachers care for lovely girls?"

"A preacher cares too much for all lovely girls to want to jest with a man about one of them," answered Camden with a smile which took the sting from his reproof.

Addison laughed.

"How queer preachers are! I don't

believe you felt that way in college. By the way, I thought you meant to study law?"

"I did study it. I gave up quite a good practice to preach."

"I've heard that it was easier to preach than to practice," observed Addison with a grin.

Camden smiled. He supposed it ought to do him good to meet one of his own kind after these years of exile, but he had been out of touch with them for so long, and somehow, with the remembrance of Mag's face in the moonlight, Addison's flippancy jarred on him.

"I'm afraid you've lamed your horse worse than you thought," said Addison. "I went to look at him. You may have to stay with me a few days against your will."

"It is not against my will now," said Camden. "With your horse injured, perhaps fatally, and mine lame, I seem led to remain here."

"Do you trust everything to luck in that way?"

"If you call Providence luck, I do. I thought it was my duty to go on to Henley's to-night, and I tried. But I was stayed by a more powerful Will than my own. I met a forlorn group of humanity whose eyes pleaded with me for sympathy. Such a call is not to be withstood."

"Do you know, old fellow," said Addison leaning forward and knocking the ashes from his cigar, "I think, in spite of all my nonsense, that you are an awfully good sort. I know what you mean by that. Even I have seen that dumb look in the eyes of some of these poor creatures that made me feel that I ought to give them something besides money. It's generally in the eyes of the women. Now you are the kind to understand what they need. Poor starved creatures. I'm deucedly sorry for them."

"Their souls are far worse starved than their bodies," said Camden.

"I only catch about half your meaning," answered Addison. "It's a lingo I don't understand. There was an awfully pretty girl once, who was taking a post graduate course, and who talked to me like that. I did n't understand what she meant either. I could n't see why such a pretty girl should be spoiling her eyes studying. Her looks would have carried her through. She talked about souls. I did n't know how to take her, so I did n't take her at all. It would have been better if she had n't known so much. But you would have got on with her."

Camden wondered where that pretty girl was, who knew about souls, and was studying. He sympathized with her for having tried to make Addison understand her.

"Yes, I would have got on with her,"

he answered. "I never meet that sort of woman any more."

A conversation like this always disturbed Camden. He wondered if it were not his duty to encourage Addison in his sympathy for these people, to rise to a higher point of view. But in spite of being a preacher, he had a horror of exercising his prerogative at inopportune times. He had seen much harm come from men endeavoring to be instant out of season. He himself could look back and remember with a vivid and ever present sense of terror, certain years of his boyhood which were mostly given over to dodging a certain preacher, who beset his way to school, and who took every opportunity of meeting him in the midst of his fellows and publicly inquiring after the welfare of his soul. In such manner many worthy men sow seeds of hatred for the very religion they represent, in the minds of the sensitive and shrinking. Thus, although brought up in a home atmosphere in which he inhaled religion with every breath he drew, Camden, in his younger manhood, came to loathe its every attribute and swung as wide of it as if he never had felt its existence. However, when his first soul-stirring sorrow held him in its mighty grasp, he fought against the return of his heart to its allegiance with an obstinacy and doggedness which had written themselves in indelible lines upon his strong dark face. But early training and the unconscious roots of his mother's religion planted in his soul when he learned Bible tales together with his alphabet and nursery rhymes, rose out of his dim past with a fervid strength which mocked his worldliness and overpowered it. His new subjection was as great a surprise to himself as to everybody else. When he succumbed, it was at once and forever. And being a radical to the very core of his being, it was only natural to his turn of mind that he should adopt this new-old religion as his calling.

But his intense humanity, the standard of self which he set for himself to gauge the emotions and endurance of others, stood him in good stead. He groped through his own sensations to those of his people. He put the Golden Rule to a new and grateful use. Within certain bounds he was all things to all men, adapting himself to their limitations and tastes with unerring fidelity, and winning many a worldly soul to a higher life through his own knowledge of the worldly.

There was a curious mixture in Camden's make-up, of which he himself stood in some awe, confident that within bounds, it was of advantage, yet uncertain, if he loosed its bonds, of where it might lead him. This was the shifting, invisible boundary line between superstition and faith, for in spite of his legal turn of mind, and the utter reasonableness of his whole nature, Camden possessed the strong, pure, boundless faith of a child. Camden's faith was even stronger than a child's, because a child's is capable of being shaken, and Camden's had passed through storm and stress and had come out with a temper and virility which would stand any strain.

The tremendous sweep of Camden's intellect took in the danger of his tendencies. At times he swung to extremes, but for the most part he held himself well in hand. To those who knew him indifferently well, his actions were sometimes inexplicable, and even appeared weak or obstinate. Thus to Addison, when in the very teeth of a storm and against all reason, Camden insisted upon crossing the levee in a vain attempt to reach his destination, saying fearlessly that he was led to do it, Camden appeared both superstitious and obstinate.

When he came back, rain-sodden, it was only his dignity and the terrible force of his quiet upon Addison which prevented him from thinking Camden ridiculous. But here Camden's faith stepped in and made him know that his leading had been to Mag in her great need. So sitting there in the night with Addison's light chatter in his ears, Camden was silent with a great peace and a trust more fervid than ever.

"That's the end of my third cigar," said Addison, presently. "Shall we turn in?"

"You go on. I'll be there directly."

The next morning Camden's face was not more haggard than usual from a sleepless night. He and Addison were off bright and early for the Manley's to see the horse.

Camden's mind was full of Mag's bravery. He was so accustomed to giving, that to be the recipient of this heavy burden of obligation weighed upon him. How brave she was! How brave and how modest!

He hoped to discover some way in which he might benefit her specifically. He took from his saddle-bags a beautiful, but well-worn copy of "Lorna Doone" and put the first volume in his pocket.

They found Tobe outside and allowed themselves to be taken to look at the horse.

The intelligent creature was standing in a tumble-down shed, with a trough on a three-legged stool before him, and a bucket of water quite out of his reach. Both of his fore legs were bandaged. He turned his beautiful eyes upon his master and neighed a welcome.

"Is he badly hurt?" asked Addison quickly.

"Hurt? He was most killed. I went after him last night after the rain, and I thought at first both his legs was broke and I'd have to shoot him."

"Shoot him!" exclaimed Addison incredulously. "It's lucky for you that you did n't."

He went closer to the horse and struck him a smart blow to make him step. He limped plainly. Tobe went on.

"When I see that he could walk some, although he was limpin' bad, I started fur home, ridin' Ol' Nick and leadin' yore hoss. We had to go powerful slow, fur Ol' Nick was in his meanest temper at bein' took out at night. He does hate to get shet of his rest. He was n't feelin' pretty no way, an' yore hoss seemed to make him feel wuss. He sort of suspicioned that he 'd been took out along o' him, so the first good chance he got, he lit out with his hind legs and kicked like all creation. Never touched yore hoss, but thowed me clean off, and eased his mind, like. It does do that mule mo' good to kick at somethin'! *He* do n't care whether he hits anything, but if he can fix things so's he's standin' on his head and his hind legs in the air, looks like to me he's mighty near happy—that is, ef mules ever do git happy.

"Well, as I was a' sayin', Ol' Nick never kicked yore hoss, but yore hoss didn't keer nothin' fur that, but ups and kicks Ol' Nick and made him squeal now I tell you. I was so mad at the cuss fur thowin' me, I was plumb glad of it, 'cept that to-day I see he is so lame I can't use him. That's him under that tree. I give yore hoss his stall.

"I do reely b'lieve my arm is sprained so's I can't work for a month. My old woman done it up fur me, but I laid awake and groaned all night. I tell you it was a powerful bad night's work, but I done the best I could. 'Taint every man would have laid up his best mule and sprained his own arm and worked hard all night for a Yankee."

"Yankee money is as good as any other, is n't it?" asked Addison.

They glanced up as they heard footsteps approaching, and saw Mag. She returned their greeting with some constraint, then turned to her father.

"What's your arm tied up for?" she said.

Tobe shifted his gaze uneasily and slowly reddened.

"He sprained it last night when his mule threw him," said Addison.

Mag kept her steady gaze on her father.

"I aint hearn tell of no sprain," she said. "Your arm wasn't tied up at breakfast."

"You could n't 'a been noticin'," said Tobe, with angry red lights coming into his small eyes, which were set too closely together to betoken honesty.

Mag looked at Addison's horse.

"And what is the matter with his hoss? I heard you telling Maw——"

"Mag, Mag!" screamed Mrs. Manley from the back of the house.

"Ma'am!" answered Mag.

"Come and tend to your churnin'! What kind o' butter do you think you'll git ef you go traipsin' off the minute you set eyes on a young fellow that's got no eyes for you."

This last, though not intended for Addison's ears, reached him quite plainly.

Mrs. Manley stood at the top of the flight of steps leading from the house to the ground. Her face was dimly discernible at the other end of her sunbonnet tunnel, and a thin wreath of smoke curled from the pipe between her teeth. The shrunk and scanty folds of her limp gown clung to ankles which in no way added to her beauty. She talked volubly during her daughter's slow approach.

Camden's sympathy was enlisted for Mag, when he saw the mortified expression of her face and recognized how she had vainly tried to frustrate her father's petty rascality. His indignation at the deception was soothed by the remembrance of the deep debt he owed Mag, who in spite of not appearing to recognize it herself, had undoubtedly saved his life.

"I don't see what is to be done," Addison said, turning to Tobe after Mag and her mother had disappeared, "unless you will take care of my horse till he gets well."

"Well, I kin tend to him. I aint no slouch of a hoss doctor, and I kin cure him. Not that it aint a bad case — a powerful bad case, but I am equil to it. I kin hobble the mules, and let yore hoss have this place till he gits well. Oh Lordy! my pore old arm!"

A swift moneyed transaction took the pain from his arm. Addison was half vexed, half amused.

"It's powerful warm. Have a glass

of buttermilk before you go!" urged Tobe hospitably.

"With pleasure," answered Addison.

As they walked towards the house several hogs grunted under its cool shadow. It stood so high that a man might stand under it without stooping.

"Oh Maw!" called Tobe. The lady answering to that name appeared. "Kin you give these gentlemen some buttermilk?"

"In co 'se I kin," she said. She indicated to Tobe that he was to go around and come in the front way, but Camden, knowing that Mag was in the kitchen, frustrated this design by marching up the steps, which trembled at his weight, without further formality.

"Company always did make Maw skittish," said Tobe, watching his wife with interest.

She was in all parts of the room at once, clattering everything which would clatter, and endeavoring to be airy and graceful in dispensing her hospitality.

"Hush your mouth, Tobe," answered Mrs. Manley, using the skirt of her gown to dust a chair with a coquetry worthy of a better cause. Mag stood by the motionless churn watching her mother's vivacious movements helplessly. Mrs. Manley sidled up to her with a playfulness quite irresistible.

"That's right, stand still and wish. The butter'll come if you only wish hard enough. You aint got a bit of git up to you, Mag Manley!"

She pushed her aside.

"What air you hidin' behind your back? A book! I thought so! No wonder the butter won't come. Were you a-readin' aloud to it? Were you tryin' to eddicate it?"

Mag flushed and shrunk under her mother's raillery, but said nothing.

"Mag aint much on talkin'," said Mrs. Manley apologetically to her visitors. "She aint much like me 'n her Paw no way you can fix it."

She took the cover off the churn.

"Why, the butter's come!" she cried, "Why did n't you tell me, numskull, stiddier standin' there like you was deef and dumb. That's just like Mag. She gits her work done as sly an' quiet and lets me scold her fur not workin' when it's all did and she knows it. She is the most onsocial human I ever see. She goes moonin' off in the woods, layin' on her back an' listenin' to 'sounds she hears,' she tells me. 'What kind of sounds,' sez I. 'The trees kin talk, and the birds have a meanin' to what they sing,' sez she, crazylike. I made out to look at her tongue, an' I gave her a big dose of quinine. I suspicioned she was goin' to have a run of fever. She aint a mite like me. I never had no eddication and I done well enough. I'm sociable, I am, but Mag don't keer for nothin' but books.

Here's Raff Patterson an' Ben Green both dyin' to court her —"

"Maw!" said Mag. She was braiding her fingers nervously together. That one remonstrance seemed wrenched from her against her will.

"You see," complained Mrs. Manley. "She won't even let me talk to a stranger when she knows I don't get ary chance 'ceptin' at protracted meeting. *I*'m proper glad to see you though if Mag aint, and the best in the house aint none too good fur you."

She cast reproachful glances at Mag, as she thus deftly turned a compliment, while instilling into her daughter's mind the rules of hospitality. She took the butter from the churn as she talked, in her excitement working her long, bony arms like pump handles.

Mag was standing at the open window with her back turned to the room, to conceal her chagrin at being publicly discussed before the gentle folks composing the great world beyond her ken, which was symbolic to her of the culture and refinement and knowledge for which her whole nature yearned.

Mrs. Manley having brought the one china cup their menage boasted, thrust a gourd into the churn and filled it with a flourish. Then she turned Mag around as if she whirled on a pivot and pressing the cup into her reluctant hand, playfully pushed her in Addison's direction. She was so evidently suffering under the stress of circumstances and the lash of her mother's tongue, that even he saw it and was sorry for her. He glanced at Camden, and saw that his eyes were following Mag with an earnestness which he did not understand.

She moved towards Addison with slow, unconscious grace, and as he rose to take the cup from her supple brown hand, he noticed that she flushed and looked at Camden.

"That's right," broke in Mrs. Manley again with asperity, "do n't say nothin' when you give a gentleman buttermilk. Just shove it at him and trust to luck that he 'll know enough to drink it. You 've fed hogs, Mag Manley, till you aint got no manners at all."

In spite of fearing to hurt her feelings, Addison broke down at this and burst into helpless laughter in which Mrs. Manley was not slow to join.

Mag shrunk from the words as if they had been a blow. Camden saw her close her teeth over her lip to hide its quivering. She was terribly shocked at her mother's want of deference to her visitors, but nothing awed Mrs. Manley.

The two men rose and thanked the Manleys for their refreshment and heartily praised the buttermilk. They shook hands with each of them. Mrs. Manley watched Mag unaffectedly give her hand to Mr. Addison, with strong disapproval. When it came her turn she drew back consciously, wiped her hands on her skirt and advanced upon him as if she were a ship under full sail. Addison received her with an effusion that was not feigned. Seldom had he been so amused.

But Mrs. Manley's object lesson to her daughter was entirely wasted. Mag had approached Camden, looking into his somber eyes deeply. He closed his hand over hers for a moment, while they looked at each other without speaking.

"Tell Mr. Addison that his horse is all right," whispered Mag.

"I will," he answered with a quick smile lighting his dark face.

The Manleys all stood at the door to see them go. Camden glanced back once. The other two had disappeared, but Mag was still watching.

Chapter IV.

"LORNA DOONE."

STILL natures with the power of self-repression developed beyond all other faculties are often misunderstood. When Mag wandered off alone to spend hours watching the haunts of bees or the habits of blue-bottle flies, her parents called her unsocial, and never questioned what she learned or thought. Yet when the first sympathetic soul crossed her path, an understanding look had flashed between them. The signs were subtle, but they were unmistakable. She was starving for sympathy. Without ever formulating it to herself, she knew that she was above the conditions in which Nature had placed her, and she longed to find a form of expression for her life.

Few were more worthy to be taught, for her thirsty mind drank in every form of knowledge within her reach. No Indian had keener sight or swifter hearing. Woodcraft and botany she knew without books. Each star in the heavens she recognized, naming the most brilliant, fantastic names of her own making. Venus was her favorite, Venus hanging low over the horizon and holding out a friendly hand to her eager little sister of the Wilderness.

Camden seemed to comprehend the life Mag led. After he left Addison that morning and took his way through the forest, his mind was filled with her. The evident need of this girl appealed in the strongest way to a nature which was accustomed to give of its bounty to all who drew upon it.

He threw himself down under a cottonwood tree to think. A pendant hop-vine, swinging its green leaves in the fragrant air reminded him of Mag's face framed in the doorway as he had looked back at her. Tobe and her mother seemed to fade from his mind. Their crudeness was apparent. It smote him with sudden pain to imagine similar vulgarity in so beautiful a creature as Mag. She seemed to him, with his spiritual insight, to be detached from the sordid poverty of her family, and to remain separate, a creature of a different sort.

As he lay there with his hat over his eyes, he heard the sad low note of a bird. Its plaint was penetrating and melancholy. It was repeated lower down, and again high up in the trees. He heard a faint rustling of leaves; a twig snapped. Presently the plaintive call was repeated, and answered from above, this time more clearly. Again a faint movement of the hop-vine, and Mag Manley crept silently into view, her hand making a trumpet from which came the muffled call that Camden had thought a bird's. Her head was thrown back and her eyes fixed on the topmost branches of a tree near by.

Mag sounded her call again, and a strange bird with iridescent plumage shot through the sunlight and lighted on a wild plum tree. Mag stood rigid, scarcely breathing. She called again and the bird answered. Her mimicry was wonderfully like. The bird looked around seeking to discover its mate. Its mournful cry and evident anxiety were almost human. When it had come as close as Mag wished, she began other bird notes, whistling, chirping, trilling like a whole forest of songsters. The hop-vine hid her from the new bird, but through its swinging, Camden could see the flutter of Mag's white throat as she poured out her volume of song. Other notes sounded from a distance in answer, coming nearer and nearer until she was only one of a chorus.

Then Mag stopped and peered out with great caution to see the strange bird's reception by the owners and inhabitants of these home woods. When a bird called singly she answered it with an ease born of long practice. Camden wondered at her patience. It seemed an hour that she stood absolutely motionless. He wanted to move, but forebore to disturb her.

Gradually she seemed to feel an alien presence. She hesitated and looked around. Then the magnetism of Camden's steady gaze compelled her, and she suddenly looked directly at him. He expected to see her start. But she held herself erect and instead of resenting his intrusion, or being embarrassed by his helpless surveillance, she appeared to include him as one who knew, and would understand.

Camden was touched by her unconscious confidence. He comprehended her attitude and realized that this was the first unfolding of a nature repressed and harassed by conditions, but which was wonderfully wholesome and sweet within.

Mag did not continue her bird notes. Evidently the spell was broken. Camden looked to see her emerge but she withdrew with as great caution as she had come. He was considerate enough of her feathered friends to wait until they had dispersed before he moved. Then he followed in the direction Mag had taken and presently overtook her.

She held in her hand the same green book that she had been reading while she churned. When she heard his footsteps she turned and waited for him. His tall figure towered even above Mag's superb height. There was something about him, in his magnetism, in the slumbering storm of his eyes, in the reserve strength of a character always at war with its own spirit, which was breathlessly overpowering. But the fineness of Mag's nature rose to meet it with exultation. The purity of her soul lay calmly in her face. Only the changeful expression in her deep eyes spoke of her longing soul.

As she stood watching Camden's approach, something within her spoke the coming fulfilment of her life. She neither reasoned nor feared. She only felt with a gladness her serious heart never had known before, that a great change was coming. She did not dream that he was the famous preacher. She only felt that this man had entered her life with a mighty sweep of power, as a Titan might descend upon a pygmy.

"I disturbed you with your bird friends," he said in strong self-reproach.

"No, I had found the one I wanted.

I had been following him up for two days. All I wanted was to see him."

She smiled brilliantly. He reached out for her book and she gave it to him. He frowned when he read its title.

"Do you like this book?" he asked.

"Not as much as I ought to," she answered with averted face. "I never knew anybody as fine as those people."

"But you like to read about them. They seem real to you. You would be like them if you could."

Camden put these questions as statements. He had a fashion of closing his lips so firmly that it made him look grim.

"And live in the house all the time?" said Mag. "Never to stay all day in the woods? To have to feel different, and think different and worry over troubles that do n't seem real? Why, *I* should n't like it. They had n't anything else to do. I aint been raised like them. You know what I am. But 'pears like they *had* to worry."

Camden looked down at her and smiled.

"Are there people like that?" she asked.

"I suppose so. There certainly are people who live in houses all the year round, who never have known in all their lives one such hour as you and I have just spent, people who live out their miserable existence fretting over needless things, and who wear themselves out in envy and following foolish fashion and fighting for money not to give away but to throw away. People who, without evil intention, leave ruin and destruction in their wake, and who, when they lie down to die, fold their hands together and pray to be saved by a God whom they have mocked with each separate day they have lived. There are plenty of people like that."

Camden spoke bitterly. Every word

was an individual shock to Mag, who had wrapped her idol in a cloth of gold and worshipped it with bated breath.

"Are they educated?" she asked timidly.

"Yes—God forgive them!" he answered harshly. "Educated in schools and colleges. Their brains are full of book knowledge."

"Are they rich?" she asked again, her face clouded with anxiety.

"Many of them. All of them rich compared to you and me. But poor and blind to the riches of Nature and the unspeakable riches of Christ."

Mag was awed.

She turned away. Camden was her first great iconoclast. He had swept aside the whole fabric of her dreams. For a moment it seemed that there was nothing to live for. If to be educated and rich and fashionable did not bring happiness or peace, and the lives these people led were condemned by Camden who had been among them and who knew, she felt that her whole aim in life had changed; her high ideals had become poor and mean, and her idols stood before her, stripped of their cloth of gold, naked and ashamed.

Camden felt her silence.

"What have I said to bring tears to your eyes?" he said swiftly.

Mag's nature rose in sudden revolt, and with Camden she dared to speak. Her habitual self-repression vanished and she spoke out with a passion as astonishing to herself as to him. Her nature in Camden had begun to find a voice.

"Then what is there left? If people who can read and understand are mean and selfish, and if riches are only wasted, and if beautiful pictures to look at and fine music to hear don't make people good and kind and noble, what is the use of living at all? I might just as well go on about my business and not try to learn and not want an education if I aint going to be any better for it after I've got it. I have always thought that ladies and gentlemen were happy because they were noble and good. But if they are not noble and good, of course they can't be happy. Only it does seem a pity to waste all these fine things on them and then not have them any happier than we are, and we don't have nothing."

Camden seemed to understand.

"This world is a large place," he said gently. He subdued his wonderful voice, which had swayed so many men and women at will, melting them to tears with its tenderness and twisting and wrenching their emotions with its every change, until Mag felt its healing touch.

"This world is a large place," he repeated, "and no two people in it are exactly alike. You and I alone in this glorious forest to-day can look at all the rest of the world and say truly, whether we believe it or not, that we are each as happy as the average man or woman in all the rest of the world. We may have our secret sorrow, which at times may overpower us, but the key to happiness lies within. We make our own lives after all. Now what you mean by lady is very different from what I mean. I have seen fair faces and white hands; I have seen fine clothes and beautiful jewels on women who were neither kind nor gentle nor sweet nor good. And I have seen worn faces, seamed with wrinkles and hands hardened and rough, and poor thin bodies, bent with work, whose best gown was a calico. But these hands had worked gladly for others. They were soft on the pillow of sickness. The feet in their worn shoes were swift to run on errands of mercy. The tired back bent again and again to do another a service. The eyes which were faded to earthly beauty were lighted from within with a light which gave them Heaven's own luster, for those same eyes had beheld the throne on high. If you asked help of the first woman, she might give you money; she might close the door in your face. If you asked help of the other, she would give you of herself, good measure, pressed down, heaped together and running over. Which should *you* call the truest lady?"

Mag smiled at him without answering. Several times as they walked slowly along, they had stood still for a moment, out of the interest they felt, and then passed on. Now Camden drew from his pocket his copy of "Lorna Doone," and asked Mag if he might read aloud to her out of *his* book. Her whole face became luminous at the suggestion. She seated herself on a fallen tree with her back against a crotch in the branches, and Camden threw himself on the soft turf. He turned the pages lovingly, as if seeking a place which would interest her, then as he glanced upward into her expectant eyes, he smiled and turned back to the first words :

"'If anybody cares to read a simple tale, told simply, I, John Ridd, of the parish of Oare, in the county of Somerset, yeoman and church-warden, have seen and had a share in some doings of this neighborhood, which I will try to set down in order, God sparing my life and memory. And they who light upon this book should bear in mind not only that I write for the clearing of our parish from ill-fame and calumny, but also a thing which will, I trow, appear too often in it, to wit — that I am nothing more than a plain unlettered man, not read in foreign languages as a gentleman might be, nor gifted with long words (even in mine own tongue,) save what I have won from the Bible or Master William Shakespeare, whom, in face of common opinion I do value highly. In short I am an ignoramus, but pretty well for a yeoman.'"

The richness and flexibility of Camden's voice combined to bring out every delicate shade of meaning in a way to make his reading of this simple paragraph promise a treat of unusual proportions. Mag completely caught the spirit of it. She leaned toward him with softly glowing face and parted lips. Hers was the unconscious grace of a wood-nymph. Her every attitude, the long flowing lines of her body were subjects for a sculptor or a painter. Her brilliant coloring, toned into faint russet shades by her life of freedom, was rich with suggestions to an artist mind. Her evident appreciation and unusual beauty stirred Camden to put forth his best efforts, which were of no mean order.

Looking at her from time to time as he read, he was well pleased that he had, as if by accident, hit upon a book so calculated to fall in with Mag's humor and taste. But Camden did not call it accident. His faith reached out after the most insignificant of trifles, for upon the least of them he had seen a whole life turn. And as he read, he unconsciously lent the superb word-painting some of his inward joy, making so wonderful a translation that Mag's pleasure was riven with a delicious pain, such as freights any new passion to a nature at once eager and high and fine.

When at last he cast the book aside and spoke to her, Mag was forced to wrench herself free, with a physical effort, from the spell his magnetic presence had cast upon her. Her color shifted and she smiled vaguely, as if the Tennessee woodlands had veritably turned to the beautiful Doone valley among the hills of Somerset. Camden would not disturb her. He only looked at her with a smiling question in his eyes.

"I understand it," said Mag, slowly answering him as if he had spoken, "with all of me." She spread her arms out and drew them together across her breast comprehensively. "I love it. How he lived — that John Ridd."

"He loved Nature as well as you do, Margaret," said Camden.

Her face quivered with feeling. He had used her full name as she never had heard it spoken before. She strove to meet the new dignity with which he invested her. She would make herself worthy.

"Only he could put it all into words," she answered, setting forth her own shortcomings with fine honesty. "Everything talks to me in just that way, only I could n't tell even you."

"You never have tried. Perhaps you could."

She shook her head incredulously.

"He saw everything wherever he went," proceeded Mag, with such evident enjoyment that Camden was delighted; "and he was not in any hurry. He always had plenty of time to stop and talk about it. Haven't you seen 'water falling from the upper rock by the means of moss and grass, as if it feared to make a noise, and had a mother sleeping?'"

Camden reached for the book in strong surprise.

"The very words," he cried. "What a memory you have. Can you go on?"

Mag colored and smoothed her dress over her knees with both hands, like a little maid at school who had been praised by her master.

"'Now and then it seemed to stop, in fear of its own dropping and waiting for some orders; and the blades of grass that straightened to it, turned their points a little way, and offered their allegiance to wind instead of water. Yet before their——'" she hesitated.

"'Carkled edges,'" prompted Camden.

"'Before their carkled edges bent more than a driven saw, down the water came again with heavy drops and pats of running and bright anger at neglect.'"

Camden's melancholy face was radiant.

"Bravely done," he exclaimed. "How do you manage to remember so accurately? It is like a photograph of the page."

"Well, I have thought things like that before, only they seemed foolish to me and I put them out of my mind. But here they sound like something fine I used to know just coming back to me."

Mag made quite an effort, for Camden's sake, in the teeth of his praise of her, to express herself connectedly and to make him know just what she meant. He appreciated it keenly.

"A great writer once said 'In every work of genius we recognize our own rejected thoughts; they come back to us with a certain alienated majesty.'"

Mag clasped her hands.

"Oh, I know," she said, with gentle earnestness. "All the way through I felt as if I had seen these same things—perhaps that I had been with John Ridd sometime."

She hesitated over this last and her face drooped. She was not used to expressing her thoughts, and her speech sounded bold to her.

"I feel that way myself often, but particularly so with this book. But you, who see so much more than I, should surely be happy in your great power of observation. I never saw anyone who saw the little things as you do."

Mag shook her head and spread out her hands with a gesture of despair.

"It is of no use to me. There is no

one to tell it to, who could understand, and if there was, I could n't make them feel it as I do. It is all locked up inside, and there it stays, going round and round and only hurting me because it can't get out. It almost makes me sick sometimes, wanting to talk to people and ask them what they think and hear what they have to say."

Mag's voice had a little ring of desperation in it, but she had given him the key to the mystery of her face.

"The wisest thought," he began slowly, searching out the roots of thought whose topmost branches Mag had stirred, "is that which is ripening in the minds of philosophers who are yet dumb. The cleverest books are those which have not yet been written. The heavenliest music is that which is still surging and beating in the hearts of men, which cannot find a voice. I have often seen faces, sometimes hurrying by me in the street, sometimes looking wistfully up at me from a sea of others, mute but eloquent with pain, faces which haunt me with the thought of what they might be, if they could only express themselves. I have seen women so melted by the sound of glorious music, and men so stirred by the sight of some heroic deed, that I have thought 'Oh, what the world loses because you do not speak now, and tell what you dream and strive and agonize to do.' Yet these same people by virtue of their sympathetic souls, the receptivity which makes them sensitive to the fine and beautiful, are the dumb poets whose silence receives the eloquence of beauty and treasures it in their hearts. They make the companions which those need who have the gift of expression. They are the great mental cushions which pillow the sharp points of speech. They are the complement of the articulate—the joy, the comfort, the everlasting haven of the speakers in this world. The sparkling eye, the tingling cheek are more eloquent than any words. The comprehension expressed by a sympathetic silence is more poignant than the most responsive speech. There is a delicacy, a fineness about an answering silence that quickens the mind beyond that which I have words to express.

"Yet if it is the silence of a dumb soul which longs for expression, I can only hope that some deep nerve-searching emotion, a grief or a joy, will shock their paralysis from them. I can not tell you how often I have heard you cry before—the cry of those we meet day by day, whose thought is beyond their speech. The world is full of them and they weigh on my heart and bow me to the very dust in my impotence to help them.

"Some I feel sure will never attain their desire on earth. There lies their heaven, and they must wait. But with you I cannot feel so. Something tells me that your way will be made plain to you here, now. In the meantime, my child, it must comfort you to know yourself. It is hard — bitterly hard to be alone as you are, to hunger so cruelly for companionship, yet it is only for a little while. Do n't let yourself despair. You will not sit down in idleness I know, and bewail your isolation. 'They also serve, who only stand and wait.' This is your time of waiting. Have patience, for you will not be so alone always. Of that I feel confident. You are only preparing yourself for a lifework. Somewhere, somehow it will open up before you, and you will find those who are just as hungry for you as you are for them. There are friends anxiously waiting even now for you to come to them. Every day that you live, every worthy deed that you perform, every unselfish act that you do, brings you a step nearer to them, and to the perfect woman that you are meant to be. 'Oh, believe as thou livest, that every sound that is spoken over the round world, which thou oughtest to hear, will vibrate on thine ear. Every proverb, every book, every byword that belongs to thee for aid or comfort, shall surely come home through open or winding passages. Every friend whom not thy fantastic will, but the great and tender heart in thee cravest, shall lock thee in his embrace. And this, because the heart in thee is the heart of all.'"

Camden watched Mag intently as he talked, glad to find from the subtile shades of comprehension written in her face, that his theory of drinking from the deepest springs was the safest for all. He would not lead this girl through gentle intermediate stages to the highest pinnacle of thought. He lifted her at once to a height which should give her a point of view, and so instantly did she respond that her soul rose like a bird and fluttered there before him. She did not interrupt him and he went on.

"You say that you cannot put these things into words as John Ridd could. Speech is given to the many, and wise silence to the few. The world is filled with chatterboxes whose emptiness makes more noise than the fulness of the philosophers. But when you are in despair over your incapacity, think of this. 'Wise speech is that portion of our wisdom, be it much or little, which we can put into intelligible words; while silence stands for, and covers as with a mystic veil of reverence, all the insights, aspirations, accumulating experiences, formed and half-formed purposes, and all the as yet unconscious, infinite possibilities, which in their totality form the sum of our character! Who then shall say that wise silence is not infinitely greater than the wisest speech?'"

Camden smiled at the little sigh of content that Mag breathed.

"Will these things make it any easier for you to live?" he asked.

"Oh yes," she said, looking beyond him with her inscrutable inner gaze which held so much of mystery that it thrilled Camden to beseech her to tell him what she saw. It seemed to him that she just overtopped his possibilities and went a step farther into the beyond which was closed to him. It drew him after her irresistibly, as if some day she might take him by the hand and lead him into her spirit-land.

While he was watching her with apprehensive eagerness, she turned towards him, bringing herself back with an effort. His tact put her so completely upon an equality with himself that she felt an expansion within, as if certain bonds which held her were loosening, and that sometime they might be riven altogether.

"There was one part you read in 'Lorna Doone' that meant me so plain I almost stopped you to tell you about it."

"What was it? Do you remember or shall I find it for you?"

"I can tell it to you. It was after he had been describing the spring-time and then he said, 'Though I am so blank of wit, or perhaps for that same reason, these little things come and dwell with me, and I am happy about them and long for nothing better. I feel with every blade of grass, as if it had a history, and make a child of every bud, as if it knew and loved me. And being so, they seem to tell me of my own delusions, and how I am no more than they, except in self-importance.'"

If it had been a confession of sin, Mag could not have looked more apologetic or abashed. The fineness of her nature was so apparent. It was like looking into the depths of a crystal pool, still and pure and limpid.

"I only wish," he said slowly, "that I saw things with your heavenly clearness. It is a precious gift. People who live in houses all the year round, I think, can never feel things as you do."

"John Ridd didn't live in a house," said Mag, "like Lady Arabella." She cast a glance of scorn upon her poor novel and then suddenly tossed it from her.

"I'm not even going to finish it," she said.

Camden appreciated the heroic proportions of this resolve. It was a printed book and as such Mag had idolized it.

"I wouldn't," said Camden gravely. "Tell me, how do you remember words so marvellously?"

"I never have books of my own," she said. "The boys get them for me sometimes, but I always give them back and I have to learn the parts I like, so that I can think of them when the books are gone."

"Wonderful," said Camden half to himself. "To think of the educations being crammed down unwilling throats throughout the length and breadth of this broad land, and to find in the depths of the wilderness so hungry a mind as hers."

He ruminated in silence for a moment. Mag's eloquent eyes were fastened upon him with her whole gentle soul in their sapphire depths. But as Camden did not look, he remained in ignorance of what was as yet a secret from Mag herself.

Camden pulled out his watch and looked at it.

"Do you know what time it is?"

Mag glanced at the sun.

"It's about a quarter past one," she said.

"Within ten minutes of it. Margaret, you are a very wonderful little woman."

Mag averted her face as she slowly lifted herself. There were tears in her eyes.

"Come, we must be going," said Camden, stowing the book in his pocket and swinging along beside her.

"Do you want to take 'Lorna Doone' home with you?" he asked.

"No, it wouldn't be the same," answered Mag.

"Then may I read to you again when I come to your house to-morrow?"

"Oh, if you only would," said Mag eagerly.

She tried to thank him, but he stopped her and smiled. She knew that he understood all that she would say, and she walked at his side in a luminous silence, conscious of a strange dignity in her own eyes.

Chapter V.

'LASSES.

A WEEK later Camden, riding along the highway toward the store, drew rein at a singularly neglected cabin which stood back as if ashamed of its appearance.

There was an air of aloneness about the place which could only come from lack of a woman's hand. The fence, patched with palings of sundry lengths, was the only thing which seemed protective. This, although uncouth and rough, was at least whole and bore up the reputation of the house it enclosed, like a single remaining virtue.

The door stood open. The great slab of marble from the unused quarry above, which served as a doorstep, might have graced a palace, its colors were so soft and fine, save that a jagged imperfection ran diagonally across its smooth surface, marring its beauty and evidently having led to its repudiation. It lay imbedded in the clay soil — a stone which the builders rejected — serving as a doorstep for rude feet.

He intended to call for water for his thirsty horse, but no smoke came out of the broken chimney, and no movement was apparent within. The small house seemed baking in the hot sun, deserted and alone.

A solitary chicken, with ragged feathers and a hoarse, despairing cluck, appeared around the corner, and stood upon one foot with the other curled up, looking inquisitively out of one eye at the intruder. And just beyond, in a narrow strip of shade, a brown, shaggy tail, evidently belonging to a dog, was the only additional sign of life.

Camden rode forward a step and

came full into sight of an unusual group. Some four or five great dogs lay bunched in the shade and in their midst was a little child, scarcely more than a baby, fast asleep.

At the sound of an approach the dogs raised themselves lazily and blinked at the horseman. Then the child wakened and stood up. The dogs lumbered to their feet, stretching themselves prodigiously. One great, gaunt, shaggy creature was almost as tall as the child.

"What's your name, honey?" asked Camden.

She put her little fat hands behind her head and said simply,

"'Lasses."

"'Lasses. That's a queer name for a pretty flower like you. And what did they name you 'Lasses for, Angel?"

"So seet," said the child, wrinkling her face into a smile and showing all her tiny, mice-like teeth.

"So sweet! I should say you were. Where's your Maw?"

The baby only gave another smile and made no reply.

"Where's your Mammy?" he questioned, thinking that perhaps she would recognize the name of her nurse.

"'Lasses," she answered confidently, nodding her head until her yellow curls bobbed.

"Yes, I know. Well, what is the dog's name?"

"'Lasses seet," she asserted, as if he had contradicted her.

Finding that he had extracted all the information her small yellow head contained, he shouted:

"Hello, the house!"

At the unusual sound 'Lasses started. But her childish confidence in the stranger was not to be dislodged, and she smiled at him once more.

She was such a dear little thing, he tried questioning her again but her conversational powers were so limited that he gave it up. He wondered, with quiet indignation, where her mother could be. Probably she was some slip of a girl who had no idea how to take care of a baby.

The dogs sat on their haunches gravely regarding this interview with peaceful eyes. One of them rose incontinently and upset 'Lasses' equilibrium. She sat down suddenly at his weight, then struggled to her feet and with all her tiny strength she pounded him with her doubled fists, while he strove to make peace with her by licking her face with his rough tongue. But she turned her head away and struck out blindly until every curl on her head trembled.

Camden rode close to the fence to dismount, but at the first sign of such an intention all five of the dogs snarled and the hair began to stiffen on their backs.

He was nonplussed for a moment. He sat still and talked to them and they lolled their tongues again, and panted with the heat. Then to test their friendliness he made another attempt to dismount. But this time they came growling to the fence and snuffed so unpleasantly at his horse's legs that the good brute backed away from such close quarters with wolfish fangs and long lean strength.

"Well, well, you inhospitable curs, I see very plainly that I am not to be asked in. I reckon the child is pretty safe after all. Nobody would care to risk five hungry mouths like yours. Bob, old boy, we'll have to go further for both your drink and mine. Goodbye 'Lasses, my baby. Go 'long, Bob."

He pushed on up the white hot road from which the heat rose in vibrations. Bob, feeling the reins loosed, hung his head gratefully and plodded along, his parched tongue thick with the fine white dust which his shuffling feet raised in clouds.

The sun sank and a tiny breeze sprang up, but it was not enough to raise the spirits of man or beast. In the gathering twilight Camden's mind wandered back to the desolate baby he had left. He wondered how late it would be until someone came home to her. He thought of Mag and "Lorna Doone."

His pulses quickened as he remembered her deep eyes during the long mornings when he had opened up before her the new world, the real world, which all her life she had longed so passionately to know. Camden did not realize that his interest in Mag was anything stronger than he had felt for many another whom he had been glad to help in similar ways. He did not place any significance on the fact that most of his thoughts of late tended to seek opportunities in which he might be of the keenest benefit to her.

Presently a clearing in the forest at his right revealed his destination, "the store." It had no other name. It was where the mail was distributed for a radius of many miles. It had to be brought nine miles from the railroad to reach even the store, and it arrived twice a week by regular carrier; oftener, if anybody happened to be going to town.

A wide covered porch crossed its whole front. Here all the men congregated to sit and talk, or to wait for a mended plow or a shod horse, for blacksmithing was one of its appurtenances.

A barrel of apples stood near the door. Within were two counters, one containing dry goods and the other groceries. A jar of pink and white peppermint candy and one of lemon, tempted stray children almost beyond their strength, poor little souls. A coop of chickens squawked from somewhere back in the darkness, and a basket of eggs packed in cotton-seed, stood on the floor.

The men on the porch discussed the stranger in whispers as he rode into the clearing and dismounted before the door. Nobody knew who he was.

"Good evening, friends," he said. "My name is Camden."

"You aint the preacher from Nashville, air you?"

"Yes. I got through with protracted meeting down at Calvary sooner than I expected, so I pushed right on here. But I lamed my horse and I've been a week on the road. It's powerful warm."

The men seemed stupefied by the intelligence that the great evangelist, who had been not only over all Tennessee, but down into Mississippi, drawing crowds to hear him night and day, had dropped down into their midst almost two weeks before he had been expected, and nobody was ready for him.

Their minds moved slowly, and it was some minutes before Uneasiness lifted its head and stirred among them invisibly. They all felt it, before all became aware of its cause. A hoarse voice occasionally was raised back there somewhere, back of the squawking chickens, in the dark room leading out of the store.

The preacher sat on the doorstep, leaning against a post, fanning himself with his hat and talking as amiably to the silent, distraught group behind him as if he had known them all his life. He could see the figure of a girl bargaining for some calico, but her face was hidden from him by her sunbonnet.

Presently a man lumbered up, and taking Bob's bridle, led him away to water.

"Ah, that's good. 'Bliged to you, brother. Poor Bob has had a hard day. By the way, can I get a drink here for myself?"

The men lifted their heads in a puzzled way.

"Of water, I mean."

They acceded to his request with alacrity and he took a deep draught from the gourd handed him. He realized that they were afraid of him and he endeavored to set them at their ease.

"Well, what news have you to tell?"

Their countenances brightened visibly. It was the most tactful thing he could have said. It took up the thread of their conversation just where his approach had broken it off.

"You've hearn tell of the new railroad, I s'pose?"

"Oh, yes. How do y'all like the idea?"

There was a composite grunt of approval and disapproval from all of them. Camden could not tell whether they were for or against it.

"I reckon the railroad's all right

enough," said Amos Henley, postmaster and owner of "the store." He was lean and weather beaten, and the tuft of hay-colored whiskers projecting from his chin, like the pilot of an engine, gave him an air of defiance which his mild manner contradicted.

"The railroad's all right enough," proceeded Mr. Henley. "Wisht I could say as much for the fellow that's bossing the job. He is a Yankee and of course a Republican."

Camden noticed that the girl in the store started suddenly and glanced at the speaker. Then she turned her attention back to the sandy-haired youth, the eldest of the Henley brood, who was measuring off some widths of pink calico.

"But I would n't care for that," proceeded Mr. Henley, "if he was n't flyin' so high with all the girls around here. There's seven of 'em that I know of—seven, going on eight"—he added with a grin at his own wit; "that air plumb gone distracted over him. I do believe he is courtin' the whole county. He is kin to the Chisholms—you passed their place down yonder in a mighty pretty grove. His own cousin, Miss Bettie Chisholm is one of the girls they say he courted. But *I* say that more than likely *she* is flirting him. She has flirted every other boy she knows; it aint like her to let this one get away. I heard yesterday that the two Brotherton girls did n't speak on account of each claimin' that she is the one he wants to see when he calls. It's a likely fellow that sows seeds of dissension between two sisters, now aint it? He is one of these soft spoken fellows. He never talks out loud to the girls, but just snuggles down and whispers to 'em. It do n't look well. I tell you that now. It aint proper the way he goes on."

"They do say," put in Mr. Taylor

Appleton, "that he is engaged to a girl in Cleveland. Henley says he gets as many as four letters a week in a lady's handwriting. He bothered Mr. Addison about it once, and since then Addison has sent his letters clean to town to be mailed. He must get some of hers there too, 'cause Henley says there aint half as many these days. But what worries Henley the most," here Mr. Appleton winked at the assembled company, "is that they do n't never write postal cyards to each other, so he does n't know for certain shore, how things stand. A fellow that won't write on postals to his sweetheart is a mighty mean man, aint he, Henley?"

A roar of laughter greeted Mr. Appleton's pleasantry.

Henley grinned, and plucked at the tuft of hay on his chin.

"Quit your foolin'," he said. "I'd like to know what y'all come hyer for, ef it aint to get the news. You shorely do n't come for your health."

"They likewise say," put in Mr. Appleton again, with slow unction at the momentous news he was about to relate, "that there is a still in this neighborhood, and that the revenue officers know it. Them revenue officers have a powerful unpleasant way of insinuating theirseffs into other people's business, on one pretext or another, and a stranger is liable to suspicion. Now thish yere Addison might be—mind you, I do n't say he is; I only say he might be a revenue officer *and* a surveyor at the same time. 'Taint no ways likely, of course, but he is *that* insinuatin'."

The men on the porch pursed up their lips, and set their fingertips together with grave suspicion.

Camden hastened to rid Addison of this mistrust.

"You are mistaken there, brother. I

knew Addison at college, and he is just what he represents himself to be — a civil engineer. He knows no more about illicit distilling than we do."

"That is as it may be," responded Mr. Appleton, politely dropping the subject, but privately hugging his misgivings of Addison. "Zion is a God-fearing neighborhood, and it reflects on us all to have a still suspected. Nobody knows of it, if there is one."

The curious manner of the girl in the store, during this discussion of Addison, had not escaped Camden. She came out just then, and the expression in her eyes as she faced the men on the porch, struck him with a pang. Keenly alive as he was to the subtle language of the human countenance, he felt that the suffering of this girl was something that he had been called here to help.

He had wondered during his difficult journey hither, why he had felt so strangely impelled to come. Other churches in other districts were equally clamorous and equally needy, yet he had been steadily drawn to Zion, and as he read the faces of the people who would gather to hear him, he knew why.

He lifted his hat and rose to his feet as the girl passed him. She turned a weak pink and white face towards him and a quiver passed over it as she greeted him, strangely at variance with the fluted coquetry of her white sunbonnet.

"Who is that?" he asked, when they had watched her out of sight.

"Laws-a-mercy!" said Mr. Henley aghast, "that was Miss Jimmie Brotherton,— one of the Brotherton sisters that do n't speak on account of that fellow Addison. I plumb forgot that she was in there, bein' kinder flustered by your comin' so sudden, and the way some other things air goin'. May be she did n't hear, and maybe she did n't care if she did hear, but I bet I've lost the trade of the whole connection."

But Camden knew that she had heard and that she cared. He thought it quite likely that Henley had lost their trade.

"They live in that white house over yonder where you see the smoke comin' up thoo the trees. There's a lot of 'em, but you'll see the whole outfit on fourth Sunday."

This reference to his calling served to remind them to whom they had been gossiping, and another awkward silence ensued.

Camden felt it keenly. Suddenly he turned to them with a smile which lighted his dark features into actual beauty.

"Are you all uneasy because no place is fixed for me to stay?" he asked.

"Well, you see we counted that you wouldn't get hyer 'till Chewsday week and—"

"Never mind about that. Never mind. The foxes had holes and the birds of the air had nests, but the Son of Man had not where to lay his head. I am not better than my Master."

He bared his head as he spoke, and his tone struck silence upon them all.

"It aint that we all, every one of us, would n't be pleased and proud to have you stay with us, only we aint fixed good enough for you. That's all. You won't have no trouble about invites once it gets abroad that you are hyer. There aint ary man on this hyer porch would n't take you home with him and welcome," said Mr. Henley.

There was a murmur of cordial assent to this. Mr. Appleton said:

"You do our hospitality proud, Mr. Henley."

"Thank you, brothers," said Camden, "I will gladly go with one of you."

Then each man fell to wondering

who should have the honor of entertaining him. His fame made him of the greatest importance. Either Mrs. Bates or Mrs. Chisholm always monopolized the preacher, and no one ever dared to demur, but now no representative of either family were present, and the time for action was ripe. It would be no small satisfaction for somebody else to carry him off bodily, the only question was, which one should it be?

In spite of Camden's endeavor to make his new friends easy in mind, he soon discovered that some other influence was at work against his success, for whenever the hoarse voice emanated from the back room, he noticed that they all started up fragments of irrelevant conversation. He endeavored to appear oblivious to all disturbances.

"Do any of you happen to know who owns that great pack of dogs down the road here?"

There was a startled silence. The

men looked at each other anxiously, and Mr. Henley vanished in the direction of the hoarse voice.

"I aint botherin' him nor nobody else. Lem me be. Lay down them cyards. If you will stay, Henley, see fair play. Tobe, you cheat!"

There was a scuffle and the sound of a blow, then a door slammed and they heard no more.

One or two of the men on the porch paled through coat upon coat of sunburn. The great preacher pretended not to hear.

"And the prettiest little baby I ever set eyes on, lying in the shadow, asleep with all those dogs."

"'Lasses," volunteered a young man who had lately become the proud father of one whom he considered far superior to 'Lasses or any other child. "That was 'Lasses; pore baby."

"Where's her mother?"

"Tell him about it, John. Tell him

the whole story. Don't leave nothin' out. She was n't kin to any of us."

The young man who had told her name, took a fresh quid of tobacco, squared his shoulders and undertook the responsibility thus thrust upon him.

"When her Paw married her Maw," he began, "there was them that said there would be trouble, because Jeff was lots older 'n her and in no ways a good match for her, she bein' ruther high steppin' for these parts. She was pretty—just as pretty as peaches, and sing! whoo-ee! How Liza could sing!

"I reckon I do n't say too much when I say that Liza could a' had most any boy that was n't married already. But Jeff was the craziest of all. It looked like he just *would n't* let her alone. I b'lieve he would a-killed himself on her front porch if she had n't give in and taken him. Jeff was never a boy to go round with the other boys. He was quiet like; but it was the quiet of the sky on a summer evenin' before the thunder and lighnin' breaks loose. He always had a solemn look, had Jeff, and there was lots of folks that was powerful 'fraid of him. But after he got Liza, he changed. 'Peared like the sun had broke thoo the clouds. He was friendly with everybody, and his face was a sight to see. I just b'lieve he loved all creation' long of Liza. He was that proud of gettin' her, too, 'cause folks had said he could n't, and had bothered him lots about her. There was one time we thought he'd got religion, his face was so 'lifted up,' my Annie said. But at protracted meetin', when Mis. Bates asked him to go up to the mourner's bench, he looked at her real gentle, not savage like he used to, and said 'Liza's my religion, Mis. Bates.' And she never said another word to him. So he never did join the church.

"Folks watched 'em both, for there

was somethin' queer and interestin' about 'em. They was different from us, and people said Liza did n't care half so much for Jeff as he did for her, just 'cause she was always laughin' and teasin' him and he lookin' at her like she was peaches and never answerin' her back.

"Then the baby came, an' they say that as soon as it was over, Jeff rushed away out into the woods alone, where he thought nobody could see him and there he laughed and cried and wrung his hands like a crazy man.

"From the very first she was the sweetes', frien'lies' little baby you ever saw and the livin' image of Liza. She'd make right up to strangers and coo at 'em like a little dove.

"Then all of a sudden, without a word of warnin' or anybody thinkin' of such a thing, Liza run off. Some say she's been heard of in Nashville, but I never saw anybody that had reely seen her.

One man said he saw a buggy the night she went, drivin' along towards town, with a man and a girl in it, and the girl was cryin'. He did n't see good, 'cause when they saw him, the man whipped up. But it reminded him then of Liza, only he never said so till he heard she had gone.

"I declare to gracious, you 'd 'a thought Jeff was ravin' distracted. He would n't speak to a woman, not even his own mother. Some say he cursed her to her face for bringin' him into the world to suffer so. He swore he 'd kill the first man that mentioned Liza's name to him. He took them dogs that he had raised from puppies and trained 'em to bite anybody that's afoot near them palin's of his. He won't let a woman come near the child, though I bet every one within twenty miles has offered to take her. He won't let her wear any of the clothes Liza made her, but makes them himself, and does everything for her. He used to stay with her all the time but now—"

"Lem me go, I say," growled the hoarse voice again. "You need n't be afraid I'll touch him. I would n't wipe my feet on a cheat. Where is this parson of yours? I'll tell him what I think of his religion. Where is he?"

A man reeled out through the store onto the porch. He was unsteady on his feet but not helpless. He confronted Camden as he rose and the two looked each other in the eyes unflinchingly, measuring man against man.

"Now Jeff," protested Mr. Henley nervously.

Camden started.

"My friend," he said, "if you are willing, your house being near, I should like to put up with you, as long as no one expected me and I have nowhere else to go."

All the front legs of the chairs on the porch came down as if pulled by one string. Their occupants seemed paralyzed by this solution of the problem.

Jeff backed away from Camden in amazement. The great preacher to want to stay with him! He dropped his eyes and the menace left his attitude.

"If you knew what I was—" he said thickly.

"I know what you are. You are my friend, my brother, and you going to be my host. Shall we go now? Here's Bob; we'll lead him and walk along together. Goodbye to you all and God bless you."

Chapter VI.

CAMDEN AND JEFF CRAWFORD.

THE supper was of the scantiest. Jeff, as he prepared it in his half sober condition, alternated between a proud delight at circumventing all the good women of Zion by entertaining most famous preacher who ever had come among them, and the feeling that he had been in a measure, trapped. He realized that he had committed himself to a solitary encounter with a man of the cloth he hated.

Jeff's heart had been made tender towards religion, even though he never had formally accepted it, through his love for his wife. Now his hatred of it was tenfold more intense, since Liza's flight had turned his whole life into ashes. There is no hatred so bitter as that engendered by outraged love. It has a reflex action which has no counterpart.

Nevertheless Jeff's idea of hospitality was such that he would not allow himself to show this feeling if he could help it.

Camden knew all this intuitively. He owed his power and his popularity to the fact that his finger was always on the pulse of his people. His sympathies were deeply involved for this wronged, desperate man and this sunny haired child liviug here in such grim silence.

Jeff allowed him to talk to 'Lasses, and the child bore out the reputation John had forecast for her. She listened amiably to all Camden had to say, but her conversational powers were limited to the fact that she was named 'Lasses because she was so sweet. She smiled at him continually and suffered him to hold her in his arms and to kiss her curls.

Occasionally she would lean forward and watch Jeff's movements with a wistful look in her great blue eyes singularly unbabylike. It was but a passing shade, however, and soon she was smiling at the visitor again and putting her little hands up at the back of her head.

It hurt Camden to look into her intelligent face, to know that some kind of thought must be passing through her childish brain and yet to know that language was denied her. He spoke of the trees and she did not look towards them; of the birds and she did not seem to know what he meant. She knew the dogs and her father, but that was all. He wondered with horror if Jeff knew that he might be making an idiot of the child. She heard no human language and lived during the day alone with the dogs, eating when they ate and sleeping when they slept, like one of them.

His heart ached in sympathy with the

unspoken misery he already had discovered at Zion.

"I reckon I'd better bring the baby in, it's getting damp out here; looks like rain."

He went in as he spoke and sat down in a chair without any back to it. Jeff acquiesced silently and seated himself on a small blue chest with corners and locks of brass.

Soon the solemn dropping of the first great rainy tears fell on the trees outside; the whole forest shivered mournfully and then, with a steady downpour, the rain fell in torrents.

Jeff had lighted a small lamp, but the darkness increased so that he rose, and lighting a tallow dip, placed it on a high shelf where it flared and sent grotesque shadows dancing on the wall. Camden noticed that 'Lasses watched them with interest and it gave him an idea.

He put her on the floor and opening

his saddlebags, took from them several large colored prints which he used to illustrate the Sunday School lesson. He selected all those with figures of women in them. There was one of Mary holding the infant Jesus. Another of the Magdalen and another of Rebeckah at the well.

Even Jeff's dull eyes brightened as Camden tacked them on the wall. Then he took 'Lasses in his arms and pointed to the figures. He spoke of the men first, that he might not arouse Jeff's suspicions, and made 'Lasses say "man" after him. Then he showed her the women and said "Lady" and 'Lasses, with difficulty, pronounced it "Yady."

"The poor lady is crying," said Camden. But 'Lasses did not understand and only said "Yady" again, as if pleased with her new lesson.

So Camden, quite carried away by his desire to impart further knowlege, and not understanding children, put his face in his hands and pretended to cry, to imitate the weeping of the Magdalen. Whereupon 'Lasses, like most babies, lifted up her voice and cried lustily in fright and sympathy.

This unlooked-for result of his well meant object lesson deeply chagrined the poor preacher. He looked anxiously at Jeff, but Jeff only grinned in derision of his awkwardness and did not even speak.

Camden gathered the weeping baby in his arms and began to pace the floor with her, nervously jigging her up and down, as he had a vague remembrance of once having seen some woman do to a baby.

"Poor little 'Lasses!" said Camden, patting her face when she had ceased. "Did 'Lasses cry? See the poor lady cry. Poor lady."

He held her close to the picture and she imitated him as children always do and pitied the Magdalen, patting her highly colored cheeks as Camden did.

"How children follow our example," said Camden to Jeff. But he made no answer.

The pouring rain drove the dogs to seek shelter in the house. They came in meachingly as if knowing that they could not stay.

When 'Lasses saw them, she wriggled down from Camden's arms and drove all out except the largest of them, Pete. The great brutes shrunk away from her baby gestures as obediently as if she had been Jeff, with Jeff's strength back of her. Pete threw himself down at Jeff's side with a gusty sigh and 'Lasses came timidly back to Camden. Seeing him look indulgently at her, she confidently bestowed a smile on him and held out her arms with childish abandon.

"She is the frien'liest baby I ever saw," said Camden.

Still no reply from Jeff, save a lifting of his dull eyes to the speaker's face. Camden so far had been unable to elicit a single remark from him except in answer to direct question.

"Pretty, sweet baby," he continued to 'Lasses herself; then "does she look like Liza?"

Jeff sprang to his feet with an oath half choked off. Camden rose instantly and set 'Lasses on the floor behind him. Jeff came close to him and with clenched fists and fiery eye-balls glared at the preacher as he hissed:

"Never mention that woman's name to me again or I'll kill you!"

Camden looked at him without flinching, but his face was so full of an infinite pity that Jeff found himself answering it.

"I hate her, do you hear me? I hate her. If I could find her — if I knew where she was, I would go to her and with my own hands, these hands right here that I'm looking at, I would choke the life out of her. I'd kill her. That's what I'd do. I hate her. I hate the child she left to me."

Still the preacher did not speak. Jeff's head dropped forward on his chest and 'Lasses crept round from where Camden had set her and looking up into her father's eyes, she murmured " so seet " sleepily.

He did not seem to see her.

" Do you know what she did to me? I reckon they told you. My story is common talk. The whole county pities Jeff Crawford. You are a great preacher. I'm told you draw such crowds that the churches can't hold them and that you've converted hundreds. You go around and talk pretty to people about bearing trouble, you, who never had any troubles to bear. I reckon you call death a trouble? I'd give my life to have seen that woman in her grave before she did this thing. Dead? Why, I could even be glad. Trouble! What do *you* know about it? How can you have the face to preach about sins when you've always been too good to commit any; and burdens when you never had any to hear. You've no *business* to come here and speak to me of mine and expect me to listen to you."

The slow, bitter strain of words stopped for a moment. The preacher's voice made itself heard. He spoke her name again.

"Did you love Liza?"

Jeff sprang at him like a tiger and struck him, but the blow was hasty and ill-directed. Camden's eyes flashed and the color leaped to his face, for the man in him resented the blow. He reached out swiftly and caught Jeff's upraised arm. His voice was hoarse with feeling, and his words poured forth like a torrent, long pent; they rushed out with the fierceness of repressed vehemence, thick and hurried.

"Crawford, listen to me and then tell me whether or not I have a right to speak to you of your lost wife. You taunt me with being too good to commit a sin. You taunt me with preaching to the sorrow stricken, who have had no sorrow myself. Man, if you carry in your bosom a grief worse than mine has borne—if your heart lies in your breast, a great heavy leaden thing, with no feeling left in it but an ache, may God in his infinite mercy, have pity on you. *Yours* is not the wrong. Your conscience, at least, is clear.

"You loved that woman, but you married her. You had her for your wife for two years. You knew what it was to have a wife's love, and baby hands on your face. The woman I loved—loved is not strong enough. No plain words can tell of the worship I had for her.

It was a madness. I would have sold my soul to gain her. She was more to me than my hope of Heaven. To have had her for even the time you had Liza, as my wife, I would have been willing to die at the expiration of it. This woman elected to love—not me; not me, mind you, who would have given my heart's blood for her, but my brother; a delicate boy who had been the favored one all his life—a lad whom Fortune had smiled on since his birth. He got for the asking what I had worked half my life for. I should have been jealous of any man, but of my brother—all my gathering fury of years heaped itself upon him when I found that Adelaide loved him. I hated him.

"They were married. No wretch on earth was more miserable than I. I lost my health. I lost ambition. I almost lost my reason. I went away to escape the sight of them, but their bliss was continually before my eyes. They did not realize my suffering, and I suppose there never was a happier marriage, but it was built on the quivering flesh of my living, bleeding heart. They had no children. God spared me that. It so happened that my brother was forced to leave her for a long time. Kindly gossip maligned him to her. Slander grew against him, and her very soul was rent by the awfulness of the stories she heard of his unfaithfulness. I knew of them, knew that she was tortured by them, but some devil prompted me to keep my lips closed, though a word from me would have given them the lie direct. Of a fragile constitution, I watched her health give way under the terrible strain of a breaking heart. She sent for me on her death bed and questioned me with her eyes; but with the sight of her sweet face, all the anguish of love and jealousy I had gone through and fought inch by inch, rose into fourfold life and mocked me. At that supreme moment her greatest pain was at the thought of my brother's fancied treachery, and I, devil that I was, let her die with her imploring blue eyes fastened on my face; I let her die believing in his perfidy. God in Heaven! Let me forget, let me forget even now the sight of those pleading eyes!

"Her death killed my brother—he only lived a short time, but he never knew my guilt. With this double sin on my soul, I thought I should go mad. I was a lawyer then, with a practice which bade fair to be a fortune to me. I gave it up. My friends counseled, pleaded even, in vain. I wrestled in this agony of mind for months, an agony which so stamped itself on my brain that the remembrance sends a shudder over me even now. My conscience was so laden with the weight of a committed sin that it rose against me night and day and drove me like a whip in the face. I became a preacher—I left the large cities—I came into the country places, among the poor and lowly. I went from place to place, from house to house even, preaching that love which passeth all understanding, hoping to buy of the Lord with human souls won through His might at my hands, enough of His divine healing to grant me one night's peaceful sleep—one single night in which my sin does not stand by my sleepless pillow and mock me with its wide-open, fiery eyes.

"I gave away every dollar I possessed and for ten years I have lived the life you now see me in, daily and hourly begging my salvation at the hands of God. I never told my story before to any human soul. I only tell it to you because your need seems to me so great. If I can comfort your sore heart; if I can be the means of reconstructing your broken home; if I can help you to bear your own burdens by sharing with you the secret of mine, I have not spoken in vain. Tell me, Crawford, not as man to preacher, but as man to man, have I a right to speak to you of Liza?"

He stopped as abruptly as he had begun. His great, gaunt frame was trembling from head to foot with the intensity of his passion. His dark eyes burned into Jeff's and the deep color glowed in a fierce, round spot in each hollow cheek. He had overpowered Jeff and borne him down before the completer misery which he had laid bare to him. Jeff's ears were filled with the sound of his voice, but his slow brain almost refused to take in the rushing, hissing current of Camden's words. His eyes held Jeff against his will. They burned through into his soul and demanded the truth from the depths of his obstinate, dogged nature. It grew painful. Jeff wrenched his gaze away with a physical effort. Camden recognized the struggle going on and released him. His hand ached with the grip he had used on Jeff's arm, and Jeff stood with his eyes on the floor, unconsciously rubbing the place left by the pressure of Camden's fingers.

How long they would have stood there neither could tell, but Pete drew attention to himself by a whine, and there lay 'Lasses fast asleep with her yellow head pillowed on the dog's rough coat.

Jeff stooped and caught her up to him and buried his face in the limp folds of her little dress. She roused enough to smile and put her pretty pink fingers on his face. He sat down with her and she fell asleep again in his arms. Camden felt that Jeff was atoning to the child in his dumb way for the hatred he had expressed toward her.

The two men sat in unbroken silence, each so occupied with his own thoughts that they forgot the lapse of time. Jeff's slow mind was absorbing the story he had heard and adjusting it to his own case. He eyed the great preacher's down bent head furtively. He dimly felt how great had been his sympathy to move him to tell his story thus, and as his eye met Camden's, a great wave of pity swept over him, and without knowing why, he rose and hastily thrust the sleeping baby into Camden's empty arms.

"God bless you, Crawford," he said brokenly.

Jeff stumbled against the blue chest as he turned away and he stood looking at it. Then he knelt down and raised its lid.

"Look here," he said, "see how she planned to leave the baby. Look at all the little dresses she made, big enough for her yet. Look at this and this. God! I could almost forgive her for leavin' me quicker than I could forgive her desertin' 'Lasses."

Jeff buried his face in his folded arms on the edge of the open chest.

"I often wonder what the child was born for," he broke out again. "Not that I don't love her. But perhaps I could forget sooner, if it wasn't for 'Lasses. She looks like her. She acts like her. She laughs like her. And sometimes I hate her for it. Yet it isn't her fault, pore little thing. She never did anybody a mite of harm. Why should she have been sent into the world to grow up and have folks point the finger of scorn at her? Tell me that. When she gets old enough to go to school, the other childern will maybe ask her where her mother is. She'll have to be told. It will break her little heart. Childern have feelin's. I want to know what she was born for? There is no place for her in all this big world. There is no place for you, 'Lasses, little daughter. It would be better if you hadn't come."

"No one is born without a purpose," said Camden gently. "This little yellow haired baby was sent to do some good to you. She holds you back from many things that you might do if it wasn't for her. And then, Crawford, did you never think that maybe 'Lasses will bring Liza back to you?"

Jeff's head was up instantly and a dull flush overspread his sunburned face as he said:

"Do you think I would take her back now? Not if she crawled to my door on her knees. 'Lasses has no mother. 'N she never will have again."

Jeff fumbled with the little slips in the chest for a moment, then suddenly slammed down the lid and stood up.

"She's never wore one of them; not one. I would n't let her if she was cold for want of 'em."

'Lasses started up at the noise and rubbed sleep out of her blue eyes with her little fists. She did not seem to recognize Camden, but looked anxiously for a familiar face.

"'Lasses," said Jeff.

She instantly held out her arms to be taken.

"So seet," she answered, with a sleepy smile.

"So sweet, so sweet," said Jeff, hugging her.

He undressed her and put her to bed as deftly as a woman. Her yellow head, covered with loose soft rings of hair, rolled from side to side during the process, as she was so sleepy, so very, very sleepy, she—could—not—hold—it—up—any—longer.

Camden watched him in thoughtful silence. He was feeling his way through Jeff's esoteric personality to his very heart's core. Camden had come here to penetrate him, to master his doggedness, to win his very soul. As he sat studying his every gesture it occurred to him that Jeff winced under his scrutiny. Camden wondered if he were not the man the revenue officers were looking for. He knew that no one was as yet implicated, but it did not take him long to single out Jeff, at least from all the men at the store, as the only one capable of so much secretiveness. His lithe, cat-like movements, his furtive but in no way skulking glances confirmed his adaptability to his calling, if he were the man. The more Camden studied him, the more he was convinced that Jeff had something to conceal. Others might be back of it, but he believed Jeff to be the active agent in the business; furthermore, that he had undertaken it just as he was said to have got into other bad ways, from desperation and recklessness. Unluckily for Jeff, he still had a conscience.

The rain had ceased, and the two men, so totally unlike, yet knit together by the mystery of a common sorrow, sat and brooded in the ghostly shadows cast by the flickering lights.

Camden felt the relaxation of having

let down the bars which had guarded his secret, and while it brought a temporary relief, it brought also physical exhaustion. He was guilty of wondering if Crawford were worth the terrible draught it had made upon him to rehearse the story. This he choked off in its incipiency with a feeling that it was unworthy of him. He was so engrossed by his own sombre reflections that he did not notice Jeff's uneasiness.

"You said awhile back that my conscience was clear. I've been thinking it over. You made a mistake there, and I've come to the conclusion that if you've made one, why aint you apt to make more?"

"Where is the still?" asked Camden.

"Down, Pete! Lie down, sir!"

It was the only quick tone Jeff had used.

"A minute more and that dog would have been at your throat. I trained him that-a-way myself."

He paused and viewing Camden's unruffled demeanor, said with gathering fury:

"Who told *you* about the still? I did n't know ary man in the county knew Jeff Crawford had anything to do with it. *Who* told you?"

"No one told me."

The quietness of the answer might have tempted Jeff to disbelieve any other man. It never occurred to him to doubt Camden. In the few minutes that he ruminated in silence upon the extraordinariness of the situation, Camden's reputation for greatness was more firmly established in Jeff's mind than by hearing a hundred sermons. He accepted all that it meant and more. He accepted all that it implied. From that moment he blindly reverenced Camden's astuteness. He asked no questions. His faith was captured. Unhesitatingly he told him all there was to tell.

"Nobody hereabouts knows it except the dog, Pete. He tracked me there once, but I most wore him out for it, and he aint been back. Only one man that I know of, suspects me and he tried to get me drunk this evenin' at the store where I was playin' cyards, so 's I would tell. M-m-m; little does Tobe Manley know Jeff Crawford. I 'm stiller than death when drink's on me."

"The revenue officers know that there is a still near here."

"How do you know? Do they? They do n't know it's me, do they?"

"No, they do n't know who it is."

Jeff turned away and said over his shoulder,

"If you was some men, I 'd ask you not to tell on me."

"Thank you," said Camden. Then he added, "Liza would n't have liked it."

But Jeff only answered fiercely:

"That 's just why I 'm doin' it."

Chapter VII.

FOURTH SUNDAY AT ZION.

IT was the fourth Sunday in the month, the day on which the yearly protracted meeting at Zion church was to begin. Mag awaited it with unusual impatience. She was divided between her desire to see Camden again, and her ardent curiosity to hear the new preacher whose fame would stir everyone to attend.

With a persistency which her mother loudly denounced as obstinate, Mag refused the gayer colors that Mrs. Manley recommended, and clung to her idea of a new dark blue print, with a bit of white around her smooth brown wrists and at her throat. She was even touched in her point of pride for her mother's appearance, but when Mrs. Manley discarded her sunbonnet and decided to resume a more elaborate affair which she had worn as a bride twenty years before, Mag knew that it was useless to demur. It had been somewhat injured by two or three serious wettings in the flood, but Mag obediently ripped and pressed and re-tied ribbons until her mother was amply satisfied with the result.

On this Sunday morning Mrs. Manley put it on her head and smiled at her image in the glass. The bonnet recalled the first years of her married life, when Tobe was called "a peart young man," and she, "the likeliest girl in the Bottom;" when Mag, as a tiny baby with unfathomable eyes and a tangle of sun-kissed curls, was clinging vaguely to chairs and the mother-skirt in her first wavering, uncertain steps in this wide life of ours. Something smarted in Mrs. Manley's weak eyes and blurred the mirror a moment, but she hastily dashed the mist aside and turned to Mag.

"How do you like it, honey? Don't you reckon Mis. Johnson will be right mad when she sees thish yere bonnet?"

Mag thought it quite likely. She was uncertain just what effect this sudden metamorphosis would produce in Zion. She strongly disapproved, but kept a respectful silence. She made a last valiant effort to induce her mother to wear shoes.

"With that bonnet, Maw, seems like you ought to wear shoes."

"Git out, Miss Mag Manley," answered her mother, with an asperity born of the flaunting head-dress, "who all's goin' to look at my feet with thish yere head awn me?"

Mag smiled with so much patience that Mrs. Manley, moved by a sudden impulse, turned and kissed her.

"You shorely air a sweet child, Mag," she said, and through the quick tears which sprang to Mag's eyes, her mother's face, even crowned by that bonnet, looked truly lovely to her.

"And to please you," she continued, "I'll take my shoes and stockin's along and put 'em awn in the grove."

"Wouldn't you just as soon do it on the levee? It would be more private," said Mag earnestly.

"Go along with you, tryin' to boss yore Maw. Well, I'll put 'em awn wherever you say. Does that satisfy you?"

Mag did not know why she was so anxious to have her family present a good appearance before Camden, when he already had seen them at their worst. But when she thought of him, every misgiving vanished, and as she journeyed towards him her heart bloomed like a flower that had radiantly lifted its face to the sun.

Already when they arrived, the grove was filled with the neighing of horses and the braying of mules, some of which, like their own, had come thirty miles since daybreak.

Protracted meeting was the one common ground upon which the "po' whites" saw the gentry. Whole families, consisting of grandparents, parents and a dozen or more children, arrived in one wagon. Packed under the seats was an abundance of food for man and beast, and beneath the wagon-bed dangled and swung the inevitable water bucket. Mothers proudly compared babies which had arrived since the last meeting, while the babies of the meeting before, crawled and cried and swarmed around their feet.

Tobe Manley hitched his wagon at a considerable distance from all the rest as a delicate attention to Old Nick. Mag remained in it, preferring a coign of vantage which commanded a view of the big road, whence she could watch the arrivals.

People stood around in groups discussing the new preacher. They seemed a little awed at the magnitude of his promised presence. Those who had not seen him, questioned those who had met him, with a minuteness inconceivable to a city-bred person. They regarded a preacher of any sort, as little short of a prophet, and the reverence they bestowed upon Camden was truly beautiful. When, added to this, came the fact that his home was in Nashville, and that he was as highly considered in that metropolis as in the humblest village, and vague rumors floated in of his having occupied even a more exalted station, his remarkable act of staying with Jeff Crawford, seemed to them a crucifixion of self but a few degrees less than when Christ ate with publicans and sinners.

Mrs. Bates and Mrs. Chisholm were worried and anxious.

"I wonder what that man gives him to eat?" asked Mrs. Bates. "I don't believe he has had a bite of fried chicken or Irish potatoes since he came, and oh, Miz. Chisholm, I feel in my soul that Jeff Crawford has n't a feather-bed to his name!"

Mrs. Bates took off her spectacles and wiped them, blinking her faded eyes feebly in the sun. Having entertained preachers so often, she felt a personal apprehension for Camden's comfort.

"I thought of that the first thing," answered Mrs. Chisholm. She had the face of a saint. The widow's ruche in her neat black bonnet crowned her silver hair like a halo. "I know he feels drawn towards the sin and sorrow of that desolate household, and if he does that precious baby good and wins poor Jeff back from his wicked ways, he may well feel rewarded. It is wrong to begrudge him to them, and I don't, except to want him to be more comfortable."

"They say that he goes about like an angel of light," returned Mrs. Bates. "Nobody can say enough to praise him. I do wish we could have him always."

Both women sighed. They had not always lived here. Mrs. Bates had been a Miss Knowlton of Nashville. Mrs. Chisholm was from Richmond, Virginia.

They were standing so near to the Manley wagon that Mag could not help overhearing them. It increased her awe of the new preacher that he should be of such moment to the two most prominent ladies in Zion. She keenly felt her own insignificance.

The arrivals were continuous.

Addison, with Mr. Totten in a new yellow cart and his little thoroughbred which he had at last succeeded in getting out of Tobe's clutches, came rather early. Addison's nerves always were sorely tried when the plunge was made from the big road down into the gully and up into the grove where Zion stood. He savagely wondered why no one ever bridged that place. He forgot that no one ever does anything in West Tennessee that can be left undone.

Miss Pat Green, who always wore her head on one side, with a contemptuous expression for Zion people because she visited in Memphis, talked flatteringly with a gaunt young man who nervously watched the big road for signs of Miss Bettie Chisholm. Miss Pat married the gaunt young man the following spring.

The Richards family consisting of two pretty daughters noted for their complexions; a married son, who formerly had sighed in vain at Miss Sallie Chisholm's feet; a bachelor son, unhandsome, but with merry blue eyes, half-way in love with both Miss Sallie and Miss Bettie, knowing well that his sisters would be delighted should he marry either or both,—all these arrived together and were greeted affectionately by everybody.

Mr. Graves Jasper, who had offered himself successively to all four of the Chisholm girls, beginning with the two now married and gone, next including Miss Bettie and Miss Sallie and winding up with their cousin, Miss Louise Addison, twisted his long fair moustache and openly stared in the direction from which his bouquet of charmers must come.

His tall dark silent brother who, people said, would never give up hope as long as Miss Sallie married no one else, talked in a low tone to Miss Jimmie Brotherton, with whom he had been in love before he met Miss Sallie, never suspecting that she was waiting anxiously for Addison's approach.

But as each arrival was other than the Chisholm girls, their city cousin, or Camden, it soon resolved itself into everyone watching for them and wondering why they were so late.

Mag's color glowed through the tan of her cheeks, and Ralph Patterson lounged near and paid timid court to her, from which she turned in that silence which to him was worse than a blow. Tobe chuckled in the depths of his ragged beard when he saw them together.

"Raff," he said with a grin at his daughter, "how does yore courtin' prosper? When do y' all calc' late to git spliced?"

"Sho,' Tobe," said Ralph, coloring and drawing the back of his hand across his mouth. He cast a furtive glance at Mag to see how she received this pleasantry, but she had stood up and was watching a new arrival breathlessly. From the stir of expectation she was sure it must be the Chisholm girls or the preacher.

She saw Miss Bettie and Miss Sallie lifted down and stand shaking out their crisp white skirts, while their escorts drove off with a flourish, "to hitch." Worn as *boutonieres* were carefully pinned a few fuchsias. Any hot-house flower which has required care and attention to raise, is greatly prized in West Tennessee.

A smart red buggy dashed up the slope and through the grove without slackening its pace, grazing formidable stumps and escaping great trees miraculously. Everyone recognized that style of driving. Mag saw Addison go up instantly to where it stood. She saw him hand some lady down—a tall stylish girl in a clinging black gown with a bunch of the big heavy roses from the Chisholm porch at her belt. Mag smiled without envy as she saw the great care he took of this girl. Her heart throbbed exultantly; she too had known such courtesies. Mag watched her earnestly as she adjusted Addison's tie with familiarity and flicked some dust from his coat with her fan. She wondered who she was.

"That is Miss Addison," whispered Ralph. "She is visitin' the Chisholms. She is kin to 'em. Ain't she plumb white though? You kin thes bet she is a lady."

Tobe shifted his quid to the other cheek.

"Raff, I kin tell y' all a good thing I got awn that air girl's brother, if you promise fur sollem shore you won't tell."

But Ralph was not listening. He was looking at Mag, who had at last caught sight of Camden's tall figure. She was trembling with an inexplicable excitement. The color fluttered to her face in waves.

"There's the new preacher, Mr.

Camden," exclaimed Ralph following her gaze.

Mag dropped down in the wagon in a little heap, dazed by the knowledge that Camden was the preacher.

"What ails you, Mag?" asked Tobe.

"Nothing," she said hoarsely. "Go awn or you won't get a seat. I'll be there directly."

Their overpowering curiosity impelled them to follow her advice. They hurried towards the crowd gathering closely around the doors, which indicated, not the time of day, but that the preacher had come.

Chapter VIII.

THE PROTRACTED MEETING.

ZION Church stood perched on four stone supports to keep it dry. The roof sloped up narrowly on either side to the ridge-pole, with nothing to break the skyline. Its two doors stood open as if hungry, and the whole aspect was of something huddled shiveringly against the horizon.

Its interior was severe in the extreme. The hard, bare seats and uncarpeted aisles gave it a meagre look. Even the high, contracted pulpit seemed gaunt and cadaverous. Two straight aisles separated the pews into three tiers, of which the men occupied the left, the women the right, while the middle was held by those whose education had reached a point which permitted men and women to sit together in church.

Never had such a congregation gathered within Zion's walls as that which greeted Camden on this Sunday morning.

Bottomites easily were distinguished from the gentry by the way in which they entered if by no other. Some men bent forward and tip-toed their way to their seats in boots which no ingenuity of tread could render noiseless, holding their inverted hats carefully in both hands as if they were bowls of water. Others bent backward in an excess of assurance, taking steps so long that their attenuated coat-tails flapped from side to side like a stair clock pendulum. Women sidled and writhed into their places with painful self-consciousness. Just before seating themselves they arranged their toilets by giving their slat sunbonnets a lurch forward with one hand, while with the other they made a comprehensive grab at the back gathers of their skirts.

The Richards girls fluttered in like swallows and settled themselves with much frou-frou of drapery and smoothing of ribbons. Miss Sallie and Miss Bettie Chisholm, followed by their eager escorts, came in demure as nuns, and beckoned Addison into their pew. Miss Addison glided in with the undulating motion which seemed to belong to her clinging black gown and pliant figure, and sat in front of her cousins. To her cavalier's surprise she sank upon her knees and bent her face upon her hands after the fashion of Episcopalians. He looked around in an alarmed manner at the assembled congregation. He was unaware how the simple, narrow, pious Methodists would regard any such papist innovation. In his mind those forms went with incense, holy water, beads and popes. No popular demonstration of disapproval having followed, he sighed in audible relief and wiped his glowing countenance with his handkerchief.

Mag hung back in a manner most unaccountable to her mother, considering their new clothes. Mrs. Manley, out of all patience with her deliberation, finally left her and went, followed by looks of envy and astonishment, to one of the front seats on the women's side.

The grotesque and the serious, the sublime and the ridiculous jostled elbows with each other at Zion. A lost soul might be saved while young people whispered and flirted, or while the Tates and Greens piously quarreled.

Old Brother Tate and old Brother Green usually occupied the flat railings which ran out parallel with the sides of the pulpit, and the one who got ready first, pitched the hymn. There was no organ nor choir. Nor was it anything unusual for both to pitch the hymn at the same time, some half dozen notes apart, and sing it through, each clinging persistently to his own key, leaving the congregation to follow which leader they would.

The Tates and Greens in days past had intermarried confusingly. Everyone in two counties "claimed kin" to one or the other, yet this feud which had begun in a friendly difference concerning brotherly love, came to include local politics and a disputed cow pasture and finally ended in their calling each other liars. Upon which the women of the family caught it up, the various kinfolks took sides, and with each year it had steadily grown worse, until now it was a county vendetta, extending into every department of their lives.

This morning, for some strange reason, Brother Tate was not there. Brother Green could hardly believe his own eyes, but he quite plumed himself. He sat with his back propped against the wall, facing the congregation, with his long legs stretched lengthwise on the rail in front of him. His heavy shoes presented a vast expanse of sole to the view of the people, half concealing, half disclosing his loosely fitting white socks, which wrinkled sadly.

There is something pathetic about the wrinkled socks of an old man, especially if they are white.

The railing on the other side of the pulpit was conspicuously empty. But through the open windows the people saw and enjoyed the sight of Brother Tate galloping up the slope on a white mule.

Camden rose and called out in a voice which clearly reached the little old man on the mule,

"Let us praise God by singing 'Oh you must be a lover of the Lord.'"

Brother Tate was seen to dig his knees into the mule in a sudden frenzy of apprehension.

Brother Green was in no hurry, for his rival was not there. He cleared his throat, ran gallantly up the scale and had just treed the note,—oh, fatal delay! when Brother Tate clattered up the steps and jubilantly pitched the tune from the open door.

Brother Green paused with his mouth open, discomfited and surprised. Then he shut his teeth with a most unchristian snap and glared fiercely at the grinning faces of some Tate boys which mocked him from the pews. The congregation straggled in on the soprano, the men pounded out the air an octave below and called it bass, while the bookless Chisholm girls improvised a melodious alto.

Brother Tate sang lustily all the way down the aisle, where he disposed of himself upon the right hand rail just as had his rival on the left.

Mr. Tate had a face like a winter apple. He wore a linen suit and green spectacles. His hair was fleecy white and hung to his collar straight. His general benevolence to all mankind only vanished when he met a Green.

While some sister was valiantly holding onto the last note waiting until the rest could catch their breath to begin the second verse, Mr. Tate caught sight of Miss Louise Addison, and although in such plain view of the people, he renounced his hard won triumph of leading the hymn, and folding his hands before him, he fatuously gave himself up to the delight of watching her.

Mr. Tate represented one of the oldest families in West Tennessee. Having amply testified his appreciation of Tennessee girls by marrying four of them, he now felt justified in casting his eyes upon the stranger, Louise, as a possible Mrs. Tate, No. 5.

Stalwart Mrs. Tate, No. 4, had been laid quietly under the sod six months before, lying close to the feeble little Mrs. Tate, No. 3, who had been a Green. People sometimes wondered if the bitter feud existing between the two families had been healed by death, or if the other three Mesdames Tate did not occasionally crowd the poor little alien who slept in their midst. No one could detect any signs of the disturbance on the surface, if disturbance there were, for the grass waved as softly over the one who had been a Green as over the other three, and the dew and the rain fell gently upon all four alike.

Mr. Tate, who realized during his brief periods of widowerhood, that time and tide wait for no man, had, by much practice, got the period of proper grief for the "dear deceased" reduced to a minimum. It was said all over the county that "ol' Brother Tate was settin' up to Miss Louise Addison, with full intention of courtin' her if things were favorable."

His intentions had been openly discussed in the grove before church began, and now people nudged each other and smiled at his manifest devotion.

Everyone was seated long since, when Mag, abashed, humiliated and with wrenched heart, crept in and hid herself back near the door. The horrible sense of faintness which overpowered her when she discovered that Camden, her teacher, her friend, was the famous preacher, seared her very soul with shame, for it opened up before her averted eyes the fact that she loved him, loved him wholly, utterly. Her temerity shocked her. He was so far removed from her that she might as well aspire to Gabriel himself. She was overwhelmed by her unconscious sacrilege.

She heard the vibrations of Camden's voice as he gave out the hymn, and it quivered along her nerves to her fingertips. It seemed to call her to him.

She wanted to stay out there alone, away from everybody, but something irresistible drew her against her will. She never knew that it was Camden himself.

Mag looked earnestly at the lovely Chisholm girls and their cousin, and from them to Camden. They were his equals. They were of his kind. The eternal fitness of things in the little group she watched, crowded itself upon her soul with a sickening oppression. They all belonged to the same world and to each other. She could picture him going home with them to dinner, as the preacher generally did. It was only proper that he should. She was beyond the pale. She looked again at the heavenly expression on Camden's face, and remembered all that he had done, all that he had been to her. She would worship him always for that alone. But she turned her face to the hard, bare wall and prayed to die.

While the hymn was being sung, Camden sat studying the upturned faces before him. He searched for the three which were photographed upon his mental sight by their need of help. They were the quivering weak face of the girl at the store; that of Jeff Crawford, holding his motherless baby in his arms, and most of all, Mag, with her eager mind and starved soul, crying blindly for light in her darkness. Although he did not see her, he felt that she was before him.

Faces there were in plenty, with lines of suffering and care written upon them; fretful faces, weak faces, bad and good faces, and some that shone like those of the saints, but all stamped with the utter hopelessness of life. In the city these same faces would be discontented. In the country they are hopeless.

He yearned over each one of these people personally. He longed to put a ray of light into their lives which was not there now. He implored that he might be able to extend their narrow horizon; to teach them to believe more understandingly, and to understand more believingly. If only he might *do* something for them!

He rose in the tall pulpit and waved the whispering congregation into silence.

"Let us pray."

The shuffling of heavy feet, the froufrou of women's gowns, the rustling of starched skirts, the fluttering of fans, the whimpering of fretful children melted away before those outstretched hands and hushed themselves into breathless stillness. There was an electric silence in the air which drew the people together involuntarily. Camden's uplifted face was radiant with divine light. His lips moved a moment in silent prayer, and the solemn quiet made itself felt upon the people like a benediction.

Then his voice was heard.

The words of his petition doubtless have faded from the minds of his hearers, but the breathless hush, his earnestness, that voice which melted and trembled and all but broke with feeling, which penetrated the depths of their callous hearts, which searched and quivered along their nerves with a force men vainly call magnetism for lack of a better word — all these will be remembered until memory itself fails. He pleaded for a surcease from earthly, bodily pain, from sufferings of the heart and mind, for anxieties and burdens to be rolled away. There were hushed pauses between the words, forcing an anxious solemnity from them, a solicitude for his solicitude, reacting on themselves and begetting a personal uneasiness for souls which were of such moment to him. There was such intimate feeling manifest in his voice, it was as if a father were pleading for safety for his own sons and daughters. He seemed to call them each by name.

Mag sank upon her knees as the solemn words dropped impressively from Camden's trembling lips.

"He is praying for me," she murmured brokenly. Her heart was eased insensibly. Camden's silent prayer already was answered. He had touched the secret sorrow of one human soul in that congregation before him.

The rustling of the people raising their heads did not disturb Mag. With her face turned to the wall still she knelt.

They sang another hymn. The waves of melody floated out on the summer air, mingling with the whispering leaves and then trembled into a vibrant silence. Mag listened with closed eyes, letting the atmosphere of peace enfold her spirit gratefully. And it was not until Camden rose to begin his sermon that Mag ranged herself out of his vision to listen.

In the pulpit Camden was most impressive. Although of a keenly nervous temperament, his manner was dignified and slow, but hinted of such repressed power and possible vehemence that these qualities subtly communicated themselves to the people, as the sensitive can feel electricity in the air.

He was of unusual height, with square lean jaws and high cheek bones where vivid spots of color concentrated under excitement. His hair was black and abundant, and he had a leonine fashion of tossing it from his forehead with a backward movement of his head. The gestures of his long arms and strong, sinewy fingers were powerful. They remained in his hearer's mind as a part of the point they bore upon. After once seeing him it was impossible to forget him. He thrilled upon the memory like a shock.

If any of his people ever wondered why it was, that with his superior education, and the evidences to the careful observer that his earlier life had been passed under different social conditions, he did not offend the vainest by his unconscious display; if they ever hazarded a guess how he so easily bridged the distance between his life and theirs, between them and him, not even the explanation which Jeff Crawford could give of the preacher's strange confidence would have been satisfactory.

It was that Camden's bitter experience had taught him that at best, poor human nature is the same the world over, and he knew that the weakest had done better than he. True humility disarms the poorest vanity, and Camden's eagerness to relieve distress struck through the thin armor of their pride as a good lance will strike through tin. He was absolutely genuine and he made them feel it. After that, everything was easy. If one will only bend low enough, one may go through the lowest portal.

The sermon was long and impassioned. Children played noisily in the uncarpeted aisles. Men got up, went out to quell disturbances among the horses and creaked back to their places.

Once when chains jangled and the squealing was unusually spirited, Tobe and Ralph went out precipitately. Their angry voices floated in through the open windows and mingled with the tender words of the preacher, striving with the unregenerate souls before him.

But in spite of Camden's powerful pleadings, there were no signs of an awakening. People seldom warmed up during the first service, which was largely one of curiosity and mental adjustment. The interest usually manifested itself on Sunday night. Nevertheless it seemed that there was a tense feeling among them, as if they felt something stirring invisibly in the air.

Suddenly a low sob smote on their ears—a voice from the women's side, back near the door. The sound produced that rustling of expectation among the congregation that the wind makes in a cornfield. Everyone turned and looked curiously, but whoever it was, shrank back and cowered down out of sight.

Camden called for the mourners to come forward, but no one came. Some one began to pray just as Brother Tate started a hymn. Neither would stop, and the hymn and the prayer progressed together.

Camden hesitated. He afterwards remembered that moment of delay as one who studies the little things of life. Then he made his way to the sobbing voice. As he bent over to take the hand of the kneeling girl, he was confronted by the luminous eyes of Mag, with an appeal in their sapphire depths which stirred his soul to respond. There was something strangely familiar in their expression. They were the eyes of Adelaide, but without the reproach in them which had so tortured him. His very heart stood still. He controlled himself with a violent effort and after a short delay he led Mag forward, with her face hidden in her hands. And as he walked with her the length of the aisle, he experienced the first dawning sense of relief which had come to him during his ten years of self-scourging remorse. He waited breathlessly for it to be withdrawn, but it remained cool and calm and high. He hardly dared believe his own sensations.

When he reached the altar, he fell upon his knees, and with Mag's hand in his, he poured forth such a prayer, such a storm of mingled thanksgiving and petition as never before had been heard in Zion church.

The effect was electric. Groans were heard, inarticulate cries, broken pleadings and snatches of hymns, and in a moment Zion was in the midst of a revival which shook her to her foundation stones. Mourners pressed forward by the dozen. The whole congregation swayed towards the front. Tears rained down the faces of strong men, and timid women prayed aloud.

Ben Green rose and was swept towards the altar with the rest. Ben was converted every year on the first Sunday of the meeting, but at night; to everybody's surprise, the frivolous little Miss Jimmie Brotherton followed him. She looked pleadingly at Addison through her tears. He felt uncomfortable. Miss Sallie Chisholm leaned towards him and whispered that Ben Green was ahead of time. He looked at her in surprise. for he himself had been strangely impressed. Instead of replying, Addison seized his hat and strode out of the church, for fear of doing something which afterwards he might deem foolish.

Chapter IX.

MAG AND 'LASSES.

IT was much later than usual when the last people left the church. Never before had there been such an awakening at the first service. Women who had had many years experience in these things, thought that such a powerful beginning argued well for the success of the meeting, and already some hopes were expressed that it might run into the second week, as the fervor decided the length of it.

The men threw curious glances at the Manley wagon where Camden had elected to dine, preferring to partake of a frugal meal under the benediction of Mag's eyes, to accepting any of the numerous invitations hospitably urged upon him by his more prosperous members.

He did not understand the change in her appearance. Her tears were gone. They seemed to have burned away with the inward fever which stained her cheeks. She held herself aloof from him, and was nervously active in helping her mother. Camden watched her apprehensively. Her splendid vitality fascinated him. But all her former manner with him had changed. Her speech was locked. She answered him in reluctant monosyllables.

Mag's mother, while deeply impressed by the honor of having the preacher dine with them, was nevertheless rather overpowered by the greatness of it. She was sufficiently abashed to discover that it was the preacher with whom she, in her ignorance, had made so free, to suit even Mag's high standard of propriety.

But now Mrs. Manley was keen to be

off visiting the neighboring wagons to exchange gossip and to show her clothes. She wondered how she could manage it without seeming rude. She looked forward with horror to an afternoon spent in the oppressive society of her silent daughter and this grave preacher, whose eyes, as she confided to Tobe, burned into her vitals like coals of fire. But as Mrs. Manley always had persisted in thinking that her vitals were situated back of her ears, this remark had a metaphorical significance to Tobe, and passed unchallenged.

Urged therefore by these combined forces, after the dinner had been disposed of, she took her courage in both hands and spoke to Camden. She was oddly nervous before his kind glances and he pitied her embarrassment.

"Ef y' all want to wrastle in prayer," she began and stopped. Camden looked at her encouragingly, but she was forced to swallow violently before she could proceed.

"Ef y' all want to labor with Mag and give the Holy Spirit a chance to work in her sinful heart, and they do say it works better in private, me 'n her Paw mought walk about and give y' all a chance. Meanin' no onpoliteness."

Camden forgot her nervousness and exclaimed:

"'Her sinful heart!'"

He meant to say more, but stopped just in time. His peremptory voice made Mrs. Manley leap with fright, and as she afterwards explained to Tobe,

"He give me such a turn I could n't rightly make out for a minute whether I was awn my head or my heels. I 'd as lives spend the evenin' with a jumpin'-jack as a man that hollers at you like you was deef and scares the sense clean out of you."

Camden, all unaware of his fault,

turned and smiled at Mag. There had been such a lifting of the habitual earnest gloom of his face that she had laid it to the effect of his powerful sermon upon his own heart.

"This dear child," he said gently to Mrs. Manley, "is already one of the Lord's chosen. I should rather ask her to pray for me."

Mrs. Manley gasped. What if Mag, with all her queerness, should turn out to be a prophet or a missionary! It would be worse than living in the house with witches. She clutched at Tobe's arm and dragged him away without further ceremony.

She had the satisfaction of being deeply envied during that afternoon, and of hearing much admiring comment concerning the new clothes. People questioned her as to what it portended. Nothing less than Mag's wedding, surely. She maintained a mysterious but knowing silence when they openly discussed whether Ralph or Ben would get her.

They strongly disapproved of Ben's continual backsliding and annual redemption, and urged upon Mrs. Manley's consideration the fact that Ralph's ugliness was only skin deep, and ought not to weigh against his worldly possessions, which consisted of a choice drove of hogs and a mule, unhandsome, but steady like its owner.

They discussed the frequence of the rains, the miasma exhaling from the Bottom in thick fogs, and the awful cases of malaria already beginning. They commented without enthusiasm, but with serious appreciation, upon Camden's untiring visits and efficient help in all the distress he encountered. But they were more poignantly interested in what he had said during dinner, what he had eaten and how he had acted. Mrs. Manley was able to satisfy their curiosity on every point, going into such details and causing him to figure in conversations, which, if he had heard them, would have set his teeth on edge.

Camden and Mag were talking quietly together upon a fallen tree plainly within view. Mag's distant manner did not repulse him. He was wrapped up in his new thought. He clung persistently to the fact that Mag's expression contained the forgiveness of Adelaide. If only she could have been Adelaide. But what if—! The new thought shocked him. His conscience rose up and smote him for allowing his vain thoughts to lead him so far away from his sacred, thrice sacred work. He felt himself grow red and embarrassed and tongue-tied.

Mag was relieved when he left her. She thought the afternoon would never pass. Camden, adapting himself to the sweet old-fashioned words, had announced "Preaching again at early candle light."

Mag sat through the evening service with grim self-repression. People viewed her askance because she did not participate in the increased excitement around the altar. The lights flared, insects swarmed in through the open windows, even an occasional bat blindly swirled through the air, but Mag heard and saw in silence.

The long ride home across the levee was peopled with crowding thoughts. She remembered that it was here she had met him. He said she had saved his life. He had come every day to their house, reading, talking to her, lending her books. He had taught her how to apply her wonderful knowledge, to express herself, to hold long conversations with him, and if, more than all, he had unconsciously taught her to love him, was she so much to blame?

Her heart cried out that it was too much to bear. He had been to her the open gate of Paradise. If now, because she was so far beneath him, because she was not a lady, in spite of his gentle remonstrance with her when she said so, she must give him up, and with him all hope of a wider life, the dead level of the future spread itself out before her clad hopelessly in gray. Until this morning she had not known that she loved him. She only knew that life had suddenly become a song.

A sharp pain in her heart made her gasp for breath. There are those who think that a heartache does not mean physical pain.

Mag laid awake long after the murmur of voices in the next room had ceased. From her bed she could see through the open window the still sapphire night-sky, that dear sky which had bended above her and befriended her all her life. She had commended to its silent trustworthiness all her hope of happiness. To-night it looked at her with such pitying eyes, it brooded over her with so much tenderness that her soul was hushed to rest as if one should say, "Sleep thou, while I watch for thee."

Each day as she sat under Camden's preaching and felt the keenness of his interest in her, it grew harder for her to wrench her heart from the love which filled it to overflowing, and turn her interest to her soul's salvation. Mag had believed all her life, but she was looking for some upheaval to take place, such as Saul of Tarsus experienced, before she could yield to the idea that she was accepted of God. Her gentle obstinacy in holding herself back from the peace she might have, sorely disturbed Camden. And it was not until, in an access of despair over her needless anxiety and suffering, that he said he almost wished that Saul's conversion had been left out of the Bible because people stupidly persisted in demanding one exactly like it, that Mag consented to believe that she was snatched as a brand from the burning.

Her face, when she realized it, was suffused with a soft tenderness that made Camden look at her in wonder. He never knew that love and renunciation had been warring in her heart all these days. He never knew that she had been waiting for her rebellious young life's consent to take up her cross.

Mag often wondered at the curious chain of events which had led her to this pass. She felt that she was capable of more active unhappiness than before she became articulate, yet she held herself bravely. The nights of anguish, the days of repression, she covered with the mantle of silence, and shrouded in that majestic garment, before whose sable folds praise and blame alike are dumb, she walked with firm step and uncomplaining eyes.

Since that first Sunday morning she had not shed a single tear. She would walk for hours with her hands gripped together and her misery visible in every tense line of her face and figure. She did not seek to explain why it came. Indeed Mag was so far from the power of analyzing emotions and motives that she might have been happy were it not that she seemed created to bear the burdens of others. There are those rare souls whose sorrow is never of their own making, whose lives might bask in sunlight except for the shadows that others cast.

Mrs. Manley watched her narrowly. Mag's smile was even rarer and more still, but there was an inscrutable something about her that forbade questions. What she felt lay in her heart too deep for tears.

Only once she wondered what was to

become of her and that was when she began to see things in the forest which she knew were not there, and to hear voices calling her to follow them she knew not whither.

She had been in the depths of the wilderness all day alone. She put her hands to her head in alarm. It felt hot and heavy. She tried to think which way to go but found that she did not know where she was. She stood still dizzily for a moment, and through the unbroken stillness came the faint distant barking of dogs. Instead of being frightened as usual, she went towards them. They sounded friendly, and although they were Jeff Crawford's dogs, they held their peace at her approach, as if they did not resent the intrusion of anything so timid and so piteous.

She knew where she was now. She could see 'Lasses through the fence. At the sight of the yellow haired baby, a heavy sob rose in her throat and she held out her arms to the child imploringly.

'Lasses, usually so timid with women, came towards her slowly, as if drawn by the yearning in Mag's eyes. Mag watched her with keen anxiety, fearing that she would turn back.

It seems sometimes as if children knew just when their heavenly healing is needed by helpless grown people, for what else can explain their sudden bursts of affection, the love expressed in their clinging kisses on such an occasion as this?

'Lasses came to the fence and looked shyly at Mag a moment. Then she smiled confidingly at her and remarked,

"Yady."

It was the one word in the English language which could have wrenched the whole of Mag's secret from her. She burst into a flood of tears and smote her hands together in impotent anguish.

"No, no! Not a lady, 'Lasses darling," she whispered, kneeling down as close to the child as she could, and clinging to her little dress as if its very touch contained healing. She drew a fold of it through the bars and kissed it, pouring out her tears upon it like rain.

"Not a lady!" she kept repeating brokenly, "or he might have loved me. When he loves, it must be a lady, you know, 'Lasses."

"Yady," asserted 'Lasses again.

"Oh, little darling," cried Mag, reaching down her face, "kiss me for that blessed word of yours. Am I a lady? I wish I was. But I'm not, oh I'm not. What's the use of pretending!"

"Yady ky," observed 'Lasses, her own face beginning to quiver at the sight of Mag's vehement crying. Then whether she understood Mag's words, or the invitation in her pleading face, she promptly gave the desired kiss, although it was bestowed with some difficulty owing to the unsympathetic and unyielding fence.

Mag took the little face between her two hands and pressed burning grateful kisses upon it, which 'Lasses returned with almost equal fervor.

"Yady ky," reiterated 'Lasses with growing anxiety. There was intense baby sympathy in her voice and it crept into the very depths of Mag's bruised heart. It was the only human sympathy she had received and all that would have been acceptable. She could talk to 'Lasses and the dogs as she could to her trees and flowers. For the first time she could allow herself the luxury of crying openly, knowing that with only friendly baby eyes upon her, she would neither be mocked nor ridiculed.

It even comforted her strangely to hear 'Lasses call her a lady, which she did assiduously in her unavailing efforts to dry Mag's tears.

'Lasses put her little hands through the bars and patted Mag's face as Camden had taught her to comfort the pictured Magdalen. In the divine unconsciousness of innocent childhood she comforted the pure and the guilty woman alike. Only culture and wisdom would later teach her where to sooth with stones and where with kisses.

So she touched Mag's flushed cheeks with her baby fingers and in a final gush of sympathy, at her wits' end for the words her little soul was bursting to express, she assured Mag that she was "so seet," and broke into helpless sobbing.

Nothing could so effectually have dried Mag's tears. She sprang up.

"Don't cry, 'Lasses," she whispered, looking around fearfully. "Don't cry."

Mag stopped and listened. Surely she heard someone coming. The dogs too were snuffing the air expectantly. Someone stopped at the front gate at the other side of the house, and she heard it click. That was enough. Although she hated herself for leaving 'Lasses in tears, she turned and fled. 'Lasses ran around the house to meet Camden, who exclaimed at the sight of her:

"What's the matter, sweetheart? Did you hurt your precious self?"

"Yady ky," she cried excitedly, pointing with her finger.

"Bless the child! She means the picture."

He started to take her in the house to show it to her. But 'Lasses reiterated her statement, and, dragging her hand from his grasp, trotted around to where she had left Mag.

Camden followed her with curiosity. She pressed her face against the fence eagerly.

"Yady ky," she repeated, pointing after Mag and dancing up and down with excitement.

Camden could just see the outlines of a woman's figure in the gathering twilight, moving rapidly between the trees.

He questioned 'Lasses unavailingly. She could tell no more, but she was strangely wistful all the evening, often going to the windows to peer into the darkness, as if watching for Mag to come back.

Chapter X.

HOW LIZA CAME HOME.

AMONG the crowds of people who thronged Zion church during the time that Camden held daily and and nightly meetings there, was one stranger of whom no one could give a satisfactory account. Camden scrutinized him closely and questioned in his own mind whether he were not one of the revenue officers whose presence had been expected in the community, although apparently he was there for no purpose except to hear the preacher, who was said to perform such wonders with the unregenerate. But inasmuch as Camden had, in a sense, forced himself upon Jeff's hospitality and into his confidence, he was not anxious to verify his suspicions.

At one service Jeff and the stranger sat in the same pew, each unconscious of the other's identity.

Camden never rose and faced his congregation without expecting to see Liza. He felt sure that she would come back sometime. He knew that the glitter of her life would wear off, and he looked to 'Lasses as the magnet which would draw the mother-heart in her back to her home. He thought it not unreasonable that she would select a time when a great crowd was gathered, hoping to come near enough to see Jeff or the baby, even if she dared not present herself openly.

Before many days his hopes were realized, and he saw her hollow eyes fixed imploringly on him from the deep tunnel of her sunbonnet. He encouraged Jeff to bring 'Lasses to the meetings, as he wanted Liza to have the fullness of her desire at once and see them together. This Jeff seemed willing to do. So it came to pass that the yellow head of 'Lasses often made a spot of sunshine in dim Zion, and Liza, watching her baby with anguished yearning, wept and prayed that the good Lord would allow her just once more before she died, to lay her poor thin fingers on those soft curling rings of hair and to press one more kiss on that little scarlet mouth.

All the women loved to watch 'Lasses. They made inarticulate motherly sounds of endearment and nudged their neighbors to look at her. And 'Lasses, feeling herself noticed, smiled peacefully at them over the back of the pew.

One night Camden and Jeff were walking home from the evening meeting and it was late. The service had been intensely exciting and Camden was exhausted. Even though Jeff carried 'Lasses, he was forced to moderate his pace to suit Camden's.

"Jeff," said the preacher, in a tired

voice, as they neared the house, "let me lean on your arm. Thank you. Did you notice a poor woman who sat behind you and cried so bitterly when we received Margaret Manley into the church? Do you know who she was? No, don't walk so fast. I see that you suspect. Crawford, she has been here many times. She is greatly broken, and her repentance is surely a sincere one. She does not ask you to see her. All she begs is that you will let her see the child. Ah, Jeff, the mother heart!"

He dropped Jeff's arm at the door and stepping into the house ahead of him, knelt down in front of the blue chest and hid his face in his long hands. Nor did he rise until Jeff had put 'Lasses to bed and had had plenty of time to think over the startling news before having an opportunity to commit himself.

During his enforced silence while watching the kneeling figure of the preacher, Crawford's mind changed from stern, angry denial to a reluctant acquiescence. Camden realized that it had required a wrench for him even to allow Liza to see the baby, so he wisely forebore to press another request home.

With the utmost discretion and a gentleness which went to her poor heart, he arranged for Liza to go at a time when Jeff was away and no intruder near to annoy her. Camden took her as far as the door himself, then considerately left her to find 'Lasses alone. But his steps were arrested by hearing 'Lasses cry out. She was afraid of her own mother. As Camden returned, 'Lasses hurried towards him with big round tears rolling slowly from her wide open blue eyes and held out her arms to be taken.

If anything further were needed to crush poor Liza's heart, this act of her baby's would have succeeded. The pitiful dress of the child, the desolate look of the house and more than all, the fact that 'Lasses could talk so little, wounded her sorely.

Before Liza left her, 'Lasses consented to kiss her mother from the shelter of Camden's arms. Who can tell the impulses which moved the child to make friends of her own accord with Mag, yet held her back from her own mother? Did her instinct tell her that there was some lack in her mother's love? Who knows?

Camden wondered if Jeff could have steeled his heart against Liza if he had seen her grief and heard what she said. But that night when he told Jeff about it, his doubts were all set at rest, for Crawford rose to almost his old pitch of violence.

"It's no use," he said fiercely, "it's against nature. No man who cared for his good name would take her back now. You see it's against nature when even her own child won't take to her.

Perhaps 'Lasses hates her. Yet why can't I? Why can't I?"

"She is very young to have a broken heart. You never thought when you married her, that she would be worse than dead, thrust out by everybody, because her husband cast the first stone?"

Jeff started up and began to pace the floor.

"Who dares to thrust her out? Does anybody, except you and me, know she is here?"

"Everybody knows it. They are not likely to let you see that they recognize her, with your threat hanging over their heads. The finger of scorn is pointed at her. She feels it very keenly and her repentance is sincere. She seems now to have but one thought, and that is that she never knew happiness except with you and that she wilfully threw it away. She feels that she has shut herself out of Paradise with her own hand, and in her sweetness and humility she makes no effort to come back." Then after a pause. "She does not seem very strong. I do not think she is long for this world."

Jeff plunged out of the house into the stillness of the summer night, as if unable to bear such words. But when he came back in the early morning, the sullen look in his eyes and his square set jaw needed no explanation as to how the battle between his great love for Liza and his outraged manhood had ended.

One day late in the second week of the meeting Camden reached a point for the first time when he wondered if he should be able to hold out to the end.

As was usual after the great strain of his success-crowned efforts, his dissatisfaction with himself and the warring of his own spirit for peace again began to rend him. It was only in the excitement and noise of the crowd, the groaning of sinners and the shouts of the redeemed that he bought a temporary release from his self accusations. He knew now how much weaker he was than when he began to live on his nerves in this manner. The drain upon his sympathies had been tremendous. It seemed to him he never had come upon more sorrows of the heart than he had encountered here. Women with tears raining down their faces whispered in his ears the story of neglect and suffering. The simplicity, the gentleness, the yearning tenderness of the Refuge he preached broke down the pride in which they had encased themselves, and men wrung his hand and blessed God that he had come among them.

After the morning service was over Camden left the church and penetrated deep into the woods, to be as far as possible from all human creatures, and by continuous prayer to purify his spirit for his last services.

He walked until he was tired, then

threw himself down under a tree to let his senses drink in the sweetness of the quiet woods. The insects droned drowsily. Occasionally a mocking-bird whistled. The wild honey-suckle swung its pink bugles in the air and made it delicately redolent. Across the narrow river bed a white path like a thin silver ribbon seemed to scale the face of the blasted rock. It used to lead to the deserted marble quarry, but it broke off abruptly now and led nowhere. Some blasting had destroyed the rest of it. The creek could only be crossed here and there, but it would be an ugly scramble up the opposite bank if any-one wished to make the attempt. Camden knew nothing of the roads here. He only had heard of the quarry path and knew that it was thought to be dangerous and was shunned by everybody on account of the unsteady condition of a great boulder which any heavy rain might dislodge.

As he lay there wondering at the stillness and absolute quiet of nature while poor humanity is so turbulent, he saw something moving on the quarry path. It looked like a dog. He watched it idly until it stopped several times and tried to go back, then turned and went on. As the path wound nearer and came out of the shadow, he saw a bright yellow spot which shone golden in the sun just over the dog's back. It looked like the head of 'Lasses—it *was* 'Lasses. How in the world did she get there? Who let her out? Where was Jeff? Above all how could he get to her?

Leaping to his feet Camden ran to the edge of the river bank and strained his eyes to see. He discovered that the dog was Pete; also that Pete was trying to make 'Lasses go back by getting in front of her and endeavoring to turn her. He kept on the outer edge of the path, however, and 'Lasses' yellow head bobbed along on the inside. The dog gave signs of fear. He pointed his ears forward and occasionally crouched down. Then he attempted to lick the baby's hands, but she fought him off and plodded sturdily forward with something of the dogged determination of her father. Camden would have given anything to know where he was, how to get to 'Lasses and how to get her home if once he got to her.

While he stood uncertain, he saw another moving object, creeping along the same path but far behind them. It appeared to be a man, but he was not walking uprightly. He was skulking along in the shadows.

All at once the situation dawned upon Camden. The quarry path led to Jeff's still. Pete had been beaten unmercifully for following him there once and was afraid to go again, but loyalty to 'Lasses kept him at her side. The man following was a revenue officer, who must have seen them start.

Just then Pete lifted his head and gave a howl of real dog misery at the painfulness of his situation. The bushes below him on Camden's side of the creek parted at the sound and a young woman stepped into view. It was Liza who recognized Pete's appeal. Before Camden could get to her, she too had seen the whole and understood its significance.

"Oh, my baby!" she cried, clasping her hands over her eyes to shut out the sight. "I know how she got there. It's easy if you know the way. See, I can get to her across here. You go back and cross there on that tree and head off the officer. Of course you know he's after Jeff. Keep him, keep him, whatever you do, till I can get word to Jeff." And she was gone, plunging down the slippery bank, crossing the shallow stream and beginning the perilous ascent before Camden had reached the tree she indicated. Twice she slipped back dangerously. He left her, straining and climbing, while he dashed into the forest and struck the quarry path ahead of the officer.

Without realizing that what he did was hindering the law, but with only the one idea in his head to save the mother and father of that yellow haired baby, Camden easily entered into conversation with him, and when he had detained him as long as possible, Camden strolled along at his side, discussing crops.

But they had not gone very far before they came upon Liza, kneeling by 'Lasses with her hands pressed dizzily to her head, and Pete was leaping around them rapturously.

And instead of tracking out an illicit distiller the revenue officer found himself helping to carry a fainting woman home and trying to staunch the blood flowing from a dangerous cut in her temple.

She was still unconscious, lying limp and white, when Jeff came in and broke down utterly at the sight of her. He knelt at her side, kissing her worn face passionately and begging her to forgive him for something.

The revenue officer looked at them curiously, for Camden's radiant face seemed to him out of all keeping with such a calamity, except that he continually paused to wipe the tears from his eyes.

When the still was raided some time later, everything was gone, either destroyed or taken away, and nobody at Zion seemed to know anything about it.

Chapter XI.

MARGARET AND CAMDEN.

ZION'S great revival was over. The story of Liza's return and Jeff's surprising act of forgiveness spread wildly, and strained every one's capacity for gossip. No one could understand how the change had been wrought and speculation was feverishly active. They heard that Liza had been hurt, but to what extent, or how, they were obliged to remain in ignorance, for although usually so swift to offer assistance, upon this occasion the neighbors held virtuously aloof from her.

Camden, who since her return, had been staying with Mrs. Chisholm, was for this reason Liza's frequent visitor. She always greeted him with a smile that took all the wanness from her sunken cheeks, it was so full of joy and ineffable content at being within the shelter of home once more. But Jeff's serenity was marred by his resentment at the aloofness of the neighbors. With open indignation he saw one after another pass his house, and he knew just how they were talking. He felt that if he, who had been most deeply wronged, could forgive her, surely they might.

Camden heard his complaints patiently. He realized their justice.

"Even Mis. Bates passed directly by here this mornin', an' tole Mis. Chisholm she ought to consider that she had daughters. I remember how Mis. Bates has been takin' awn durin' protracted meetin', rejoicin' at the backslider's return, an' cryin' over that low down Ben Green, fit to make you sick. An' she knows that Ben is just too ornery for any good use, an' his salvation do n't hardly last over night. Now look how she acts about Liza! Such Christianity aint good enough for me. I'm a heap sight better off without it."

"But Jeff," urged Liza faintly, "Mis. Chisholm come herself this mornin' an' brought them white roses an' laid 'em right hyer awn my pillow. Then she bent over and kissed me like she was n't afraid it would pizen her to touch me, an' she said in such a gentle way, 'My dear, I'm so glad you 've come back.'"

Tears choked her utterance, and Camden was forced to wipe his own eyes.

"Yes," assented Jeff, relenting. "An' she sent a loaf of her salt-risin' bread that Liza's hearn tell of all her life, an' some Sally Lunn an' rusk an' syllabub. Liza said she never tasted such good things. But the child seems to care more for them roses than anything else."

"*White* roses, Mr. Camden!" said Liza with shining eyes. A delicate color flickered into her pale cheeks as she reached a thin hand for her treasures.

"But the Johnsons aint been here," said Jeff, allowing his grievance to master him again, "nor the Pattersons, nor the Tripps."

"You aint no call to be mad, Jeff." Liza's low voice seemed to stir Jeff as irresistibly as ever.

"Patience," said Camden. "Time will heal and adjust everything."

"Nor the Manleys," Jeff could not help adding.

"Then something is wrong with them, for nothing would keep Margaret Manley from Liza," said Camden.

"Maybe some of 'em's got the fever," suggested Jeff.

"I hope it aint Mag," said Liza. "I aint quite liked her looks lately."

"Why not?" demanded Camden, with startled sharpness.

"I watched her in church. She's got somethin' the same look that Mis.

Chisholm's got. It sets proper enough awn Mis. Chisholm, havin' lost her husband, but it don't look right awn a young thing like Mag. She sets around so peaceful, with that there light awn her face, an' her big eyes a shinin' like she saw somethin' that the rest of us did n't. I feel like if Mag gets sick, she'll die. I *hope* it aint Mag."

Liza's words fell like lead on Camden's heart. Yellow fever was raging in Memphis, and one or two victims of so-called malarial fever in the Bottomland had died so suddenly that Camden's suspicions were aroused. He hesitated to speak of them, for a panic was sure to follow the first alarm. The ravages of this dread pestilence were so awful, so swift, so fatal.

Camden told them good-night hurriedly.

"Try to get strong," he said to Liza, "there may be work for you to do."

He left her looking with radiant happiness on 'Lasses' yellow mop of hair visible on the pillow, and took his way toward the Manley's. He never thought of delaying his visit until morning. Mag might be in need of him now.

She answered his knock, holding a candle above her head.

"Mr. Camden, is it you? I am so glad you have come. My mother and father are both sick, and they act so queer, I was getting frightened. I never saw the fever do this way before."

She sheltered the flame with her hand and led him into the room where the sufferers lay. One glance into their vacant congested eyes convinced him of the truth of his worst fears. He looked apprehensively at Mag, and she motioned him from the room.

"Now, what is it?" she questioned, facing him.

"Can you bear the truth, Margaret?" he said, kindly, taking her hand in his. "I am afraid it is yellow fever."

Mag's fixed gaze clung to Camden's face in silent horror.

"Then that's what ailed the Tripps," she whispered. "Everybody thought it was queer the sudden way they died, and both the same day. Mother helped nurse them. I reckon that's how she took it. Oh Mr. Camden, do people ever get well?"

"Oh yes, with good nursing, often. We must get a doctor at once. Try not to be afraid of it. I shall not leave you alone with them. Be sure of that."

Just then came a call.

"Hello, the house!"

They went hurriedly to the door. There was something menacing in the very atmosphere. The night seemed full of startling sounds. It was Ralph Patterson, who rode close to the doorstep.

"I'm goin' to town for a doctor," he said. "Mis. Johnson's took with the fever, and she is so awful sick, they are plumb scared to death. The Butlers that brought the Tripp childern home with them are down since mornin'. Is anybody sick hyer?"

"Both Mr. and Mrs. Manley," answered Camden.

"Do you reckon it's yellow fever?" asked Ralph, under his breath.

"I fear that it is."

"Oh, laws-a-mercy! Laws-a-mercy! What shall we do? Everybody that can get away will light out, and who will hep those that have to stay?" groaned Ralph.

"Don't take on so, Ralph. I'm not afraid of it and you mustn't be."

"Wait until I write some telegrams," said Camden. "I will send by you for nurses from Memphis. I don't like the way this thing has begun, but we must make the best of it. Don't frighten Margaret, Ralph. She is being very courageous."

He wrote the telegrams, and Ralph

received his instructions with his honest face quite pale and harassed. They watched him ride off at full speed, with his lantern swinging on his arm.

This was the beginning of weeks of dreadful pestilence and horror. A panic seized everyone. Within a few days, all who could, had taken their families and fled from the scourge that swept so remorselessly through the bottom-lands and over all that section of the country. Camden went from house to house, speaking words of encouragement and comfort and sympathy, but constantly returning to help Mag nurse her father and mother.

Mrs. Manley died first, but Mag held herself bravely for her father's sake. Camden's whole soul was filled with her silent sorrow. Now that necessity chained him to her daily presence, he felt his heart warm toward her with a new and unwonted tenderness. But his uncompromising honesty of purpose would not suffer his mind to be diverted from his round of duties, and he dared not give himself up to the comfort this feeling brought him. It seemed to his clairvoyant mind that she had erected a slender barrier between them which was not there in the beginning, so that even when her father's death left her utterly alone in the world, Camden felt that he could not speak to her as he would.

When the plague spread so that towns were quarantined, and it was difficult to get the barest necessities, heroic deeds of matchless bravery walked silently beside acts of insane cowardice and selfish terror. The nurses Camden sent for did not come. Yellow fever spread to such an extent in Memphis that they scarcely could care for their own sick and were forced to beg assistance from the north. These were days of sorrow and heart-break and woe unspeakable. Almost every house wore the garb of mourning.

In this emergency two women stepped into public view, almost hand in hand, asking Camden to send them wherever they were most needed. They were Mag Manley and Liza Crawford.

For a moment his human selfishness bade him withhold Mag from such a deadly danger. While he might have been able to encourage and support Liza's resolve, it seemed to him that he would be sending Mag to certain death. He gazed at the sad beauty of her face, softened, dignified, ennobled by the strange forces which were at work in her life, and said hesitatingly:

"Are you sure you are not afraid?"

"No, I am not afraid of anything now."

Camden was seized with a sudden longing to turn the isolation of that pathetic "now," into an immediate realization of his hopes and desires. Her resignation strengthened his apprehensions for her.

"Are you strong enough, Margaret? It is such exhausting, weary work. You — you look pale to me."

The smile with which she strove to reassure him was sadder than her tears. Her throat ached with the smothered sob that would rise at the way he seemed to concern himself about her. She wished he would not. It only made it harder for her. She felt that she must do something, anything to take her thoughts away from her sorrow and the loneliness which now stretched before her more hopelessly than ever. To be sure there was Ralph. Turn which way she would, there was always Ralph, worshipping her dumbly, clinging to and drawing on her sympathies in a way which made her almost desperate with a fear of what she, in a moment of weakness, might be forced to choose.

But even if she did. She thought of herself and Ralph together, hopelessly together, and then of the empty, empty years.

"Are you trying to prevent me?" she asked, raising her eyes to his with a baffled look. "I *must* go now. I am needed. I must have work. Oh, let me go, Mr. Camden!"

Liza, who was going immediately to the Johnson's, stood listening.

"Let her go, Mr. Camden," she urged. "It will hep her. She'll be better off."

The grim repressed look, which Mag remembered to have seen when she first knew him, returned to Camden's face. She had missed it gratefully of late. It always gave her the miserable feeling that the man was scourging his own spirit, that he was closing the bars against the human to make room for the entrance of the divine. In such moments the woman-heart in Mag seemed resistlessly drawn towards him by his inner suffering. It was the heavenly compassion in the great motherhood side of humanity that stirred in her. All her soul was in her eyes, if Camden had but seen. She conquered herself with an effort.

"Where shall I go?" she asked.

"If you must go," began Camden, with a note of desperation in his voice, "go to Mrs. Patterson's. Ralph is worn out, half-sick himself and broken-hearted with the fear of losing his mother. The way that boy loves her is beautiful."

This demand, meeting her at the very outset, almost closed Mag's heart against all suffering but her own. It was the finger of Fate pointing to her doom. To be in Ralph's daily presence was to see the toils closing relentlessly around her. It made it worse that it should be Camden who sent her there. Liza Crawford, though not clever, being a woman, saw deeper than Camden. She saw Mag move her head restlessly, and caught the troubled, hunted look Mag flung at her.

Camden, watching her, thought she was re-considering her resolve.

"You think better of it? You will not go?" he said, eagerly.

Mag looked at him. It was a large, dilated, wondering look, before which his greater intelligence and wider knowledge shrunk. The blood tingled in the palms of his hands. He wanted to kneel at her feet and beg her forgiveness.

Her only reply was to make ready to go. Camden went with them, yet he dared not speak of his misconception of her. They rode in silence until they reached the Patterson house. Its forlornness never struck Camden so keenly as when he saw Mag's womanly dignity within its walls. She seemed to fill the place with her presence.

Ralph's amazement at the heavenly good fortune which, in his darkest hour, had fallen to him out of the murky clouds, filled him with a speechless comfort.

Camden could see how Mag's gentle electric personality permeated the little dwelling like a breath of spring wind, putting new life into Ralph's weary frame, and lighting the dulled eyes of the sick woman, whose one hope in life was to live to see Mag her son's wife. Camden and Liza helped her to settle in her new abode, saw what she needed and got an idea of her environments. They left her at last with a strange reluctance, both looking back at her as she stood in the doorway to see them go.

"That's what I call brave," said Liza, drawing a deep breath.

"And is n't it just what you are going to do?" asked Camden.

" No, indeed. Mine's a heap easier,

for there'll only be one thing for me to work against. But Mag will have something that she dreads worse than the fever."

"And what is that?" said Camden anxiously.

"It's Raff. He's been courtin' her ever since she put awn long dresses. He's always loved her. She do n't keer nothin' for him, but she's afraid she'll have to take up with him, now that she's left alone. I do n't mean that anybody's goin' to make her marry him, but she's dreadin' the way things have turned. It looks like the finger of God, sendin' her there and me to the Johnson's, when it just as easy could have been the other way."

Camden looked as if his faith in this evidence of the finger of God was strangely weak.

"Why did n't you tell me this sooner?" he demanded.

Liza looked up, startled by his tone.

"Why, I reckoned everybody knew that Raff Patterson was courtin' Mag Manley. You might have seen it if you 'd looked, or been thinkin'. But never you mind, Mr. Camden. Maybe she will get to lovin' Raff, bein' with him so much, for as you said, he is a sweet boy, an' the way he loves his mother is just beautiful."

"I only feel that it is too bad to try Margaret beyond her strength," answered Camden.

Liza's face softened with a dreamy smile.

"It does Mag a power of good to hear you call her Margaret. She always has held her head a leetle high, considerin', an' it makes her feel that you have a different notion of her when you call her Margaret."

"How can you tell, Liza?"

"Oh, by her face. Mag never did say much, but if you watch her face you can tell pretty much what she 's thinkin', 'cept when she goes too high. She can get a look that I can't follow. But when you say 'Margaret,' she draws herself up, an' raises her head, an' somethin' comes into her eyes that makes 'em bigger an' bluer an' shinier. 'Pears like to me there's a light all over her face."

Liza seemed to have a shrewd, woman's notion that she was interesting the man beside her. She said more than she had intended and more than she ever had succinctly thought out before, led to do it by the expectant silence of Camden, which urged her. But with her deep reverence for the preacher, it was beyond her thought that he should love Mag, who, like the prophet in his own country, walked unknown and unrecognized in their midst.

When they reached the Johnson's, Liza little knew, as she watched the strong, swift way in which Camden brought order out of chaos for her, even as Mag had done it at the Patterson's for herself, that she had given him something strangely disquieting to think about, or that she had added a new element to his interest in Mag.

Chapter XII.

MARGARET FINDS HER OWN.

WITH a sinking heart Mag watched Liza and Camden drive away. She shaded her eyes with her hand and stared after them until they melted out of sight between the trees which overhung the road. She gave a last lingering look at the sunlight. She realized that she was about to risk her life, and that perhaps she might never again pass through the green wilderness which always beckoned her so irresistibly.

In the background of her thoughts hovered Ralph. Mag could feel the menace of his presence in the very atmosphere. She went in suddenly, with a determination to face him, and have done with her foolish fears.

He must know her attitude at the outset.

It was an easy matter to chill him, but it was not so easy a task to go in and out of the sick-room of the woman whose eyes, in her rational moments, followed Mag's every movement with wistful pleading, and who, in her delirium, begged and prayed her to marry her son, in a way that sadly shook the girl's composure.

Camden came every day. Sometimes he overheard these ravings of delirium, but they never spoke upon the subject. Mag only colored painfully and averted her face. He saw Ralph following her about the house like a faithful dog. Mag held herself steadily before Camden. She would not complain, and there was something about her that forbade either sympathy or advice.

Notwithstanding her faithful nursing, Mrs. Patterson sank rapidly, and one morning when Camden came with the awful news that Mrs. Butler and her sister had died during the night, it was only to find that Mrs. Patterson had followed them, and Ralph was on his knees at Mag's feet, clinging to her gown and weeping aloud over his loss. He was nothing but a great boy after all, with a most loyal loving heart, and his mother had been his idol. It was no discredit to him that he mourned her in that childish fashion, with great tears running between his fingers and heavy sobs shaking his frame. Mag was sorely distressed by his grief. She laid a gentle hand on his head and strove to comfort him, but he only took her hand in both of his and covered it with tears and kisses.

When Camden essayed to speak, Ralph's face twitched painfully, and he shook his head, saying:

"It's only Mag can comfort me if she will."

"No, Ralph, dear Ralph, please do n't

put it on me. I've done my best, but it's no use."

Ralph flung himself down beside his mother with a bitter cry. Mag turned her pale face to Camden, and his heart bounded at her silent appeal from Ralph to him.

"You must go away from here," said Camden with decision. "I will stay with Ralph. The sun is just rising. Walk down the road, and you will meet Liza. I made her come out too. Let her take you back with her. Now go at once."

It was so good to be ordered to do something in Camden's old peremptory voice, and to know that he would take up her duty to Ralph.

So Mag went to Liza and the two women worked together. Then each went elsewhere. The dead were not even buried before they were called to another scene of desolation. Terror aided the disease, and many died of fear. But Mag and Liza, under Camden's instructions, ministered from their own fearlessness to the mind as well as to the body.

The unostentatious, daily heroism of these two thrilled Camden as unyielding courage in the weak always thrills strong men. He watched over their health and saw to it with anxious firmness that they took every possible precaution.

If, in their unselfish devotion, they did not obey him, he came and took their places while they slept or walked in the open air.

"You shall not kill yourselves under my very eyes," he said. And they were sustained by the feeling of protection with which he surrounded them.

The uplifting sense of ministry which came to them when whole families hung upon their courage and skill, gave them the inward distinction with which Self-sacrifice glorifies her own. Camden found himself relying upon their judgment, consulting with them, even asking their advice. His nerves were of steel, or he would have given out during those weeks when he was all heart and brain. He saw Mag draw doubly upon her own superb youth and strength to shield Liza's frail stock of vitality, with an adoration riven with apprehension.

The plague crawled and crept its noxious way through the bottom, leaving death and destruction in its wake, and then, as if not satisfied, reared its fearful crest and reached its long fangs towards the healthful high grounds, which might never have been visited, except for the breathless heat, and the decaying vegetation the wet season had engendered. This exhaled a miasma which invited pestilence. It seemed as if the blessed frost would never come.

With the brutal malice of anarchy, the fever chose the home of the gentlewoman, Mrs. Chisholm, as its first rest-ing place. When she saw her two daughters stricken down before her eyes, the little frail mother was no more fitted to cope with it than the delicate bit of old Dresden that she looked. The colored servants scattered like leaves in a high wind at the first alarm. Only one faithful old woman, the black "Mammy" who had nursed them both as babies, refused to leave her darlings. She stood by them heroically until she herself was stricken and died.

When Camden returned from his self-imposed services in the deadly Bottom-land, he found Mrs. Chisholm alone with her sick, fairly gasping with the horror and loneliness of her situation. She burst into a flood of tears when she saw him. He took both of her little thin old hands into his great warm palms.

"My dear Mrs. Chisholm," he said, "pray don't give way like this. You must bear up for your daughters' sake."

"But it is so terrible to be left alone in this way. I am sure Sallie is going to die. It breaks my heart to see them. I have telegraphed even to Nashville for a nurse, and I can't get one. Oh, Mr. Camden, I believe the Lord has deserted me in my hour of need!"

"No, dear soul, no. Indeed He has not. Miss Sallie is going to live. It is always darkest just before light breaks. This very day I am going to bring you a nurse who is God's ministering angel. She will make your daughters well with her good nursing, and she will comfort and care for you. It is Margaret Manley, who lost her father and mother when the fever first broke out, and you never saw so lovely and self-denying a spirit. She has gone from house to house, nursing the sick, encouraging the well, burying the dead, a veritable angel, bearing hope and healing in her wings."

"Oh, Mr. Camden, do you think she

will come? I have been disappointed so often."

"I will go after her myself and bring her to your door."

He set off at once. He could not help a feeling of boyish exhilaration at the prospect of the long drive alone with Mag, with no one to interfere with his having her all to himself. It seemed impossible to think of all the sorrow and death lurking behind closed doors, when Nature smiled so radiantly and the woods were one glorious rainbow of color.

At first Mag was overpowered by the thought of going into the house of Mrs. Chisholm to nurse those two beautiful young creatures before whom she always had fairly held her breath. But this feeling which once would have paralyzed her faculties, now only caused her a moment's hesitation and a moment's thrill. A soft pleasure stirred in her heart at the thought that Camden had come to fetch her, and that under his escort she would first set her foot in the house of the greatest lady in the county.

"I can't go just now. I must stay and finish this."

She held up a little white slip she was making to shroud a tiny body.

"Whose is it?" asked Camden, gently.

"It is poor little Annie Tripp's, whose father and mother were the first to die of this awful fever. She was so patient and sweet. It nearly broke her heart to die and leave her baby brother. She did n't seem to mind her suffering, but she kept crying 'I promised to take care of him! I promised! I can't go and leave the little fellow all alone!' She died this morning in my arms. She was delirious and thought I was her mother. She told me over and over how much she loved me, and how she loved Mag, but she burst out crying when she tried to tell how much she had missed her mother, and how lonesome it was in the dark every night. She fell into a stupor, and I thought she would never come out of it. But she opened her eyes and called me her 'dear Mag,' and wanted me to kiss her, and then—she died."

Mag buried her face in the little slip and cried softly. Camden sat beside her in silence until the simple frock was finished. Mag put some flowers in the tiny, wasted hand, as her mother would have done if she had been there to watch and bless the brave fight the little child-mother had made against the Death that beckoned her from her charge. Mag knew that she must let other hands lay her beside her mother, yet she could not bear to go. The child seemed to have taken a strange hold upon her heart. Camden waited patiently for a time, then took her gently by the hand and led her away.

To go to Mrs. Chisholm's they must cross the levee; the levee peopled with memories to them both. Mag gazed from its height into the cool, green tree tops, whose waving branches tossed the sunlight back whence it came, and left them in their grateful shade. She remembered how on another day, she had ridden across this part of the levee with Camden, yet not alone with him. Here was where she had met him. This was the very place where she had stopped his horse.

He turned and looked into her eyes. She was so tall that they were almost on a level with his own.

"I never pass this point," he said, "that I do not think of you. Let no man say that women only possess moral courage after that. It sends a thrill over me even yet when I think of your danger. I felt that I was rushing along to certain death. The horse had bolted, at his own shadow perhaps; I never knew what. I had no control over him. With his head down, and the bit between his teeth, he was running at the top of his speed along this wicked levee, where a single misstep would have dashed me into Eternity. The rumble of the wheels in my ears sounded like the roar of thunder. As people, when they are drowning, are said to think of everything in their lives at a flash, so my life passed in review before me. I felt that I was making expiation for everything; that the Lord had accepted the sacrifice of my life at last. Then I heard your shout, and my blood froze in my veins. My own danger had so completely filled my mind that I never thought of the menace I might be to others. I knew then that someone was ahead of me. I knew that at any moment I might hear a crash and I felt that all would be over and that I never should hear anything again. Then suddenly the horse stopped, and I saw you.

I found how little I had been ready to die, for no glimpse of an angel will ever be dearer to me than the memory of your face that night. And then to think that you saved my life at the risk of that precious life of yours, that is doing so much for others in life and in death! Mine was bought at far too dear a price. It was not worth it."

"You have repaid me a thousand times," said Mag earnestly. "I had never lived at all until you showed me how. Think how I was wasting my time."

"Have I done anything for you, Margaret? It seems to me that my burden of gratitude to you will never be paid off. It weighs on my heart."

"That is a little unkind to me," answered Mag gently. "I think you might accept it from me as gladly as I take things from you, with never a thought of a burden of gratitude either way."

"You are right again. As usual, you have pointed out a higher sentiment than I knew before. There is no finer generosity than to receive generously, with the same largeness with which one gives. Your nice perceptions would be a constant humiliation to me Margaret, if I did not look for them so eagerly, and glory in the fineness of your gift. There is no one in the world who shows me the beauty of life and the spiritual delicacy of its warp and woof as you do."

"As I? Oh, Mr. Camden!"

Mag felt that he had taken the very words out of her mouth and the tribute out of her heart that she gladly would have bestowed upon him. She set her lips together more firmly at the hopelessness of ever making him or anybody know what she felt. Those were the words she had been struggling to say to him ever since that morning in those very woods they were driving through, when he had read to her from ".Lorna Doone," and then talked to her of the philosophy of life as she never had been talked to before, and never expected to be again, unless on some blessed day, he might take up the theme where he left it, and lead her into the fuller, clearer light where he habitually stood. Camden never knew how many times Mag had sought out that fallen tree and lived over the hours they spent there, repeating his words to herself until they became a part of her daily thought.

To Camden it was a delight to feel that she was at his side, that just by turning his head, he could look into her face. If he dared to reach out, he could touch the hands lying together in her lap—those dear hands which had just performed the last tender offices for the little motherless child in her charge.

And Mag close by his side, did not dream that she was in his heart, but sat there with a dumb ache at the emptiness of her life. So there is nothing in telepathy after all.

When they drove into the grounds surrounding Mrs. Chisholm's house, Mag thought of the time when Camden had told her that a larger life would soon open up before her. She wondered if she might venture to speak of it to him. She was afraid it might sound arrogant or bold, so in silence he lifted her down and took her across the deep porch where so often she had seen Miss Sallie and Miss Bettie sitting surrounded by the young men who could not seem to keep away.

Alas, with all the bloom gone from their cheeks and all the light from their eyes, the idols of two counties now lay upstairs in darkened rooms, with the finger of Death upon their pale lips.

Mrs. Chisholm met them at the door, and taking Mag's tall young figure into her frail motherly arms, she kissed her tenderly, murmuring broken words of thanks and gratitude through her tears.

Mag's sensitive face flushed with pleasure, and from that time on, her only grievance was that Mrs. Chisholm did not ask her to die in her cause.

Mag seemed born to nurse the sick. She had not been an hour in the house before there were gracious, grateful changes everywhere, even in the appearance of the sick girls.

Mrs. Chisholm watched her in humble thankfulness. She was serving her loved ones. Camden had promised that she would make them well. Mrs. Chisholm, turning from watching Mag's quiet movements, surprised a look on Camden's face which told her what he never had told to Mag. She gave an instinctive start of shocked surprise, and drew in her breath sharply. She was an old gentlewoman all through. But she said nothing.

At the end of a week the sick were

out of danger, and when the doctors said it was all due to the nurse, it was not gratitude alone that made Mrs. Chisholm feel that Paradise itself would be inadequate to Mag's just deserts. Her highbred appreciation of genuine nobility had made her open her heart to the tall young creature, the womanliness in her recognizing the innate womanliness of Mag.

When Camden came again to see how he might be of further use to them, Mrs. Chisholm drew him into the cool, dim parlor where she could speak to him alone. She laid her finger on her lip.

"She is asleep, and I would n't have her disturbed for anything," she whispered.

"Is she better?" asked Camden.

"I was speaking of Mag. Thank God, both of my daughters are out of all danger, and the doctor says it is wholly due to the nurse. I can see them improve under my very eyes. He tells me now that he despaired of their lives the day before she came. Oh, Mr. Camden, what can I ever do to repay her?"

"Give her of your dear love. She has lost her own mother and she is entirely alone in the world."

"I love her already more than I can say, and she shall always have a home with me. Oh, she has done more than their own mother could have done. My love and my anguish and anxiety to cure them, hampered me. She brought more than her nursing. She brought a fresh untried mind, stored with the most unusual knowledge. Why, when they were so nervous that they could get no sleep, Mag would talk or read to them half the night. I discovered it in this way. One night I was wakened out of sleep by a laugh, a real laugh. I hadn't heard one for so long, Mr. Camden, that I started up, and my heart almost stopped beating. I listened, and heard all the birds singing in the early dawn, and the laugh came once more. I thought Sallie was out of her head again. Just then the clock struck twelve, so I knew that it could n't have been the birds singing. I thought then that I had the fever, but my head felt cool to the touch, and I seemed to know quite well where I was. I could hear strange sounds. I got up and crept to the door, and all of a sudden every bird that I ever heard, began to sing in the sickroom. I looked in, half dead with fright, and it was Mag. The lights were burning in both rooms, the girls were wide awake, and Mag was going back and forth between them, making those lovely bird-notes in her throat. When I showed myself, she explained that the girls could n't sleep, and she had found that if she amused them in this way for awhile, they went to sleep of their own accord. A few days after this, Bettie felt so well, she insisted on being dressed and sitting in a chair by the window. Mag carried her in her arms like a baby, and when she found she was too weak to sit alone, Mag held her in her lap. If I just could have had them painted as they sat there, they were both so pretty and so sweet!"

"I wish I could have seen them," said Camden. "I have heard Margaret call birds in the forest in that way. It is wonderful, the way they answer her."

"Did you ever hear her read out of her head? She knows page after page of books. The girls never tire of testing her memory, or hearing her tell stories about the habits of insects and little animals. I never saw such a girl. Sallie and Bettie are uneasy when she is out of their sight."

Camden listened with a prouder delight to Mrs. Chisholm's honest praise of Mag, than he ever had to the gracious words she had spoken of himself.

But much as he longed to take her into his confidence then and there, he was withheld by the idea that the first words of his passion belonged to Mag herself.

Mrs. Chisholm was in a tearful flutter of thanksgiving over the recovery of her daughters. Camden shared her gratitude with a devout heart, thankful that his dear Margaret had been instrumental in saving two such precious lives. But they were barely able to be about the house when their mother was stricken, and Mag's skill was again called into requisition.

Liza, who for the first time was at leisure, begged to relieve her, but Mag would allow no one in the sick-room but herself. In this house her work was truly a labor of love.

"If anyone can save her, I can," she told Camden, with stern determination in her attitude, born of her hand to hand fight with the arch-fiend. "Make

Liza rest. She needs it worse than I do."

Mag was most faithful. She seemed to know neither fatigue nor fear, though as the sorrowful days went slowly by, she looked worn and pale. There were pathetic purple shadows under her sweet eyes and fine lines of suffering around her mouth.

It was the crisis in the case. The doctor said that night would mark some change. Camden offered his services, but no one would consent to rest. The hours dragged by, weighted with anxiety.

In the gray dawn Mag crept down to where Camden waited, worn to the verge of exhaustion, but persistent in remaining awake and within call. She found him sitting by the table with his head on his folded arms. He had fallen asleep. He started up at her step, alert as ever, wakening from a dream of her. But his smile faded when he saw her tears.

"What is it? Is it all over?"

"Oh, no," she answered. "She will get well, and they are so happy over it. They have their mother left for them to love, and mine is gone. She was all I had! Oh, I am so alone in the world!"

In a moment Camden's long arms were around her, and her head pressed against his shoulder.

"You are not alone for one moment," he said, pushing back her hair and looking earnestly into her eyes. "Not for one single moment while I am alive to watch over you and love you and take care of you. I love you with all my heart and soul. Your influence has been upon me unconsciously from the first, and in the last few weeks I have come to know your newer and heavenlier heroism with a feeling akin to worship. If you will accept the life you saved that night, I humbly offer it to you. Don't speak. Don't say anything unless you can say that you love me with such a love that I must have, that I will have from you, my Margaret."

Tears dimmed her eyes, and she shook her head.

"Don't speak," he insisted, rejoicing in the flush that leaped to her very temples. "Forget what you were going to say; forget everything except that I love you. I need you. You round out my whole nature. I need you in my work to help me to see. Such beautiful eyes as you have, dear. I love your eyes. I love you."

Camden's stormy wooing overpowered her.

"I am not worthy," she murmured.

"Hush. Not one word of that kind from you to me. It is I who am not worthy of you."

He was stung to self-scourging by her inward gaze, which seemed to read his soul. "I must confess to you that

I have sinned beyond hope of pardon from God. I have consecrated my life to His service, hoping to buy forgiveness at His hands. Every soul that is saved, I fling into the balance to weigh against my sin, and say, 'Lord, is it enough?' And the answer comes back, 'It is not enough.' So I toil again and yet again. I must tell you this. Perhaps you already know it. Your eyes penetrate deeply. But you must understand and forgive. I cannot, I will not let you go. You must be more merciful than God."

Mag drew away from him, surprised, grieved, shocked.

"What are you saying?" she exclaimed. "You, trying to buy what is only meant to be given away? You, who can make others receive without money and without price—and then weigh out souls to pay for your own salvation? No matter how you have sinned, you can be forgiven. That is what you preach. Can't you believe it? Do n't you see your mistake?

In her efforts for him Mag was carried out of herself. Camden stared at her, a sudden light struggling into his face. He turned his back to her abruptly and folded his arms.

"No wonder it seems to you that God answers, 'It is not enough.' He means that it never will be enough in that way. You can never buy. He must give and you must receive. Don't you understand?"

Mag's deep, slow voice penetrated to the very core of his heart and carried a dazzling, yet absolute conviction in its train. Suddenly he turned to her, and took her face between his two hands. His whole attitude was radiant.

"You will never know what you have already been to me," he said brokenly. "You have made me see how terribly wrong and blasphemous I have been all these years. Trying to buy what is to be had for the asking! Oh, you sweet woman-soul! Do you see now why I need you so much? Do you understand me when I say that I cannot, that I will not live without you?"

She only looked into his eyes deeply. His love had so dignified her in her own sight, that she was adjusting herself to the rapture of this new point of view to which he held her so tenaciously. What a life—to help him in his work! Her dumb spirit struggled for its release. If she could but speak what she felt!

"If you only knew what you have exorcised," he cried, with a heavy sigh of relief. "For ten years I have stumbled blindly along a path beset with thorns, and all the time there was a way lying so close that it almost touched, so close that the light from it occasionally struck across my darkness, and yet I could not see. In one swift moment you have set my feet in this new path.

Now I only need your hand in mine to make my whole life stretch out before me, glorious in promise. Margaret, do you love me? Answer me."

And in Mag's answer her soul found its voice.

www.ingramcontent.com/pod-product-compliance
Lightning Source LLC
Chambersburg PA
CBHW031955230426
43672CB00010B/2154